Andrew
bookmarks

Miro
(accent on
first
syllable)
'bout
Toni
Morrison
and
Gael

ELEMENTS OF PSYCHOTHERAPY

ELEMENTS
OF PSYCHOTHERAPY

Allen J. Enelow, M.D.

Professor of Health Behavior
University of the Pacific
Pacific Medical Center, San Francisco

Director, Division of Health Behavior
West Coast Cancer Foundation

New York   OXFORD UNIVERSITY PRESS   1977

12 — 8 ~ 23

TO SHEILA

ACKNOWLEDGMENTS

The art and skill of psychotherapy can be learned only through practice, with good supervision from several teachers. Of the many who were helpful to me I should like to acknowledge in particular the patient, thoughtful teachers who influenced my work the most: Maxwell Gitelson, at Michael Reese Hospital (Chicago); Jan Frank and William L. Pious, at the Menninger Foundation; Ernst Lewy at the Los Angeles Psychoanalytic Institute; and Hellmuth Kaiser.

The students and psychiatry residents I have taught have helped me refine my ideas through discussions of their problems in acquiring psychotherapy skills. The psychiatry residents and psychology interns at Pacific Medical Center who have participated in my psychotherapy seminar have been of particular help in providing useful questions and criticisms of this and several earlier drafts of the manuscript.

Michael L. Russell not only contributed the chapter on behavior therapy but also broadened my understanding of this increasingly important approach to psychotherapy during our two years of working together at Pacific Medical Center.

My debt to Leta McKinney Adler, my behavioral science colleague of long standing, is acknowledged elsewhere in the book. She has provided me with a sociological perspective that has significantly influenced my thinking about psychotherapy.

Finally, I wish to express my gratitude to Elaine Jaynes and Shirley Jacobsen, who supervised the clerical and administrative details of the seminars in which the book was developed as well as the typing of the manuscript, to Linda Kemp, who typed several drafts, and to Mary F. Swander, who typed the final draft.

San Francisco   A.J.E.
January, 1977

CONTENTS

INTRODUCTION

This book was written for students of the health professions, many of whom will use psychotherapy in their work and some of whom may become psychotherapists. It aims to describe the elements of psychotherapy, the behavior of the therapist, and the similarities and differences among the various approaches to psychotherapy in common use. Even though psychotherapy can be learned only through practice under supervision, this book should provide the beginning therapist with a general introduction to the field and a broader view of this type of treatment than can be given by a supervisor helping the student to struggle with the problems of one patient using one type of psychotherapy.

My first attempt at psychotherapy as a medical student in the psychiatry clinic was far from satisfying. I don't remember what I said or did, but I distinctly recall my tension and feeling of uncertainty about what to say or do. There seemed to be no rules to follow in this ambiguous procedure. It was several years before I became accustomed to that. In the thirty or more years since then, I have heard many students express similar feelings of uncertainty and desire for clear-cut procedures.

The discomfort of the beginning therapist usually seems to be connected with his feeling that he has to *do* something. This leads sometimes to giving advice or direction—often without sufficient information to know whether the advice is appropriate or can be acted on by the patient—or sometimes to inappropriate probing for buried feelings or memories. It also leads some therapists to premature espousal of one or another conceptual model of psychotherapy that appears to promise a set of rules or procedures to be followed. But there are many useful approaches to psychotherapy. No one type of therapy is useful for all patients, while any of several approaches might be helpful for a given patient. Thus, it is desirable for psychotherapists to be familiar with all of them and to have had training in a number of them.

My training in psychotherapy began with analytic, insight-oriented therapy, as did that of most psychiatrists of my generation. During my psychiatry experience as an intern, then subsequently when assigned to a psychiatric service of an Army general hospital, and still later during residency training, there was a great deal of emphasis on insight and how to help patients achieve it. Though we used supportive and directive therapies, these were considered palliative measures, not directed at the cause of the patients' disorders and consequently seen as "minor" procedures in contrast to the more "important" analytic therapies. At the Menninger Foundation (where at that time—1947–1949—training was conducted at Winter Veterans Administration Hospital and at the Menninger Clinic), though much attention was given to insight therapies for outpatients, we were exposed to a variety of treatment approaches and a wide range of psychiatric illnesses: supportive and "suppressive" psychotherapy, milieu therapy of hospitalized patients, and several variants of insight-aiming psychotherapy. I had the opportunity to learn from many skilled therapists, largely psychoanalysts but with different views of psychoanalysis and of less intensive psychotherapy. These experiences helped to shape the empirical approach that has characterized my psychotherapeutic work by making it clear how many things the experts did other than interpreting the unconscious aspects of the patient's psychological functioning.

In those days, admission to the Psychoanalytic Institute for further training was the prize most sought by Menninger residents and junior staff. Upon gaining admission to the Topeka Institute in 1949, I had high hopes of learning how to carry out psychoanalytic treatment and becoming a better therapist in general. During the next six years of study at the Topeka and Los Angeles psychoanalytic institutes, both, I felt, had been accomplished. But the struggle to apply psychoanalysis to the varied problems of my patients, and the need to modify the basic procedures in dealing with different individuals, made me increasingly aware that classical psychoanalytic methods have limited applicability. Clinical and economic constraints made it necessary to see most patients less frequently than several times weekly, or to work with them in ways other than insight-aiming ones. Moreover, the diversity of views among my teachers on how psychoanalytic treatment should be carried out highlighted the fact that the application of psychoanalytic principles by each analyst is highly individual, that these principles are only broad guidelines for therapists. I saw that interpretations might be helpful to some patients but not to others, and that insight seemed to accompany improvement in some instances but not in others. And, since many patients who might have been thought likely to benefit from psychoanalysis could not afford the necessary three or four sessions a week, I had the opportunity to experiment with a variety of less intensive approaches, insight-oriented and otherwise.

Like most students, I became less interpretive during my psychoanalytic training, making fewer direct efforts to bring unconscious wishes or tendencies into awareness, and paying more attention to what Freud referred to as "the surface of the mind." In 1955 I read an intriguing paper by Hellmuth Kaiser entitled "The Problem of Responsibility in Psychotherapy," and wrote to him. This initiated a correspondence that later led to many long conversations, and a relation that lasted until his death in 1961.

Kaiser introduced me to the process-oriented "here-and-now" approach to psychotherapy. His type of therapy, a derivative of psychoanalysis, sought to create a situation that would foster the emergence of the patient's characteristic neurotic communication by giving the patient few or no guidelines for his behavior, either during psychotherapy sessions or outside them. By focusing on the way the patient interacted with him during psychotherapy sessions, Kaiser shifted the emphasis from the content of the patient's communications to the patient's behavior. After experimenting with a Kaiserian approach, once again I found that, while very often helpful to patients, it was not predictably useful.

In 1958 I began to spend a half-day each week with a multidisciplinary group at the University of California (Los Angeles) Alcoholism Research Clinic, studying various approaches to psychotherapy. The perspectives of a psychologist and a sociologist helped me clarify further my ideas about psychotherapy. Because of that experience, soon after joining the faculty of the University of Southern California in 1960 I began a long-lasting collaboration with Leta McKinney Adler, a sociologist. We studied interviewing and psychotherapy, and taught both to physicians.

One of the seminars we conducted served both research and teaching purposes. In that seminar, I treated a patient with psychotherapy behind a one-way screen, observed by students, while Adler and her assistants developed an instrument for coding the psychotherapy interactions in terms of process rather than of content. Then we held a seminar discussion with the students, after which we worked on refining the interaction analysis instrument. During the years 1961–1968, Adler and I developed the definitions set forth in Chapter 2 of the various kinds of behavior used by therapists in their work. I also worked on refining the low-inference, process-oriented style of psychotherapy described in Chapter 5, chiefly for use with patients who have neuroses or personality disorders other than those characterized by destructive or asocial behavior. I have found elements of this approach to be useful with all patients.

In 1967 I encountered the work of Albert Bandura in *Research in Behavior Modification* (Krasner and Ullman, 1966). It was my collaboration with a sociologist that helped me see its significance. Bandura presented evidence that social learning is fostered by exposure to models whose patterns of behavior can be imitated, whether or not intentionally. The concept of learning new social behavior through modeling seemed to explain why some patients' style of communication and social behavior changed during psychotherapy.

Bandura rejects the psychodynamic theories that attribute the deviant actions of individuals to powerful internal forces that they cannot control and whose existence they do not recognize. Nor does he believe that man is totally controlled by environmental influences. In his view, practically all learning that results from direct experiences can occur on a vicarious basis through observing other people's behavior and its consequences for them. People can create symbolic representations of external influences for themselves and later use them to guide their actions. People can anticipate probable consequences of their actions, can solve problems symbolically and alter their behavior accordingly, without having to experience the consequences of their behavior before changing it. Through such learning from models and observing the consequences of others' behavior, people can learn to control their behavior to varying degrees. And as people change their behavior, the response of others toward them is likely to change. Behavior that evokes positive and rewarding responses is likely to be perpetuated. Of course, genetic endowment and constitutional factors may limit the range of behavior that a given person can develop and the rate at which behavior can change (Bandura, 1966, 1971).

The therapist clearly can and does serve as a model for the patient. Then why not make deliberate efforts to model new behavior for patients? This led me to further study of social learning theory and efforts to apply behavioral methods to such problems as modifying behavior associated with cardiovascular risk factors.

Community mental health became an important part of my work when, late in 1967, I became Chairman of the Department of Psychiatry at Michigan State University. A community-based, newly federally-funded, comprehensive community mental health center was to become a major teaching site for the medical school. My first task as Chairman was to organize it. Both there and at Pacific Medical Center after 1972, I was responsible for programs in which crisis intervention and social rehabilitation were the most important treatment methods. Chapters 7 and 8 are based on those experiences.

All these learning experiences have been, and to a greater or lesser extent remain, useful to me. Consequently, I do not consider any one approach to be universally applicable. The therapist who can use a variety of methods is much more likely to be capable of helping patients with a broad range of problems than one who takes a single approach to psychotherapy. The various styles of psychotherapy described in this book should be viewed as *elements* that can be thoughtfully, variably compounded in the psychotherapy of each patient.

In the course of applying psychotherapeutic principles to a wide range of health problems, I have become increasingly impressed with the usefulness of supportive measures. I have also come to appreciate the value of patiently gathering data through facilitating the patient's telling of his own story, and of being unobtrusively supportive during the early interviews, avoiding premature commitment to a therapeutic strategy. In some instances, four or five such interviews may suffice to make the patient feel better and begin to find reasonable solutions to his problems. More commonly, of course, the patient and I come to see the scope of the problem and are then able to choose a treatment strategy with greater confidence. Beginners often fail to appreciate that merely trying to understand what a patient is saying and to help him clarify his own thoughts and feelings is therapy in itself.

I have tried to communicate this philosophy in the chapters to follow. Each approach to psychotherapy is described as being applicable to a degree that depends on the patient. But the different approaches are rarely used in unalloyed form. Most commonly, elements from several approaches will be employed. Combining insight- and process-oriented therapy may be most useful with a voluntary outpatient who has a neurosis and wants to understand himself and change his behavior. Social rehabilitation and supportive psychotherapy, on the other hand, may be most useful with a chronically psychotic patient.

The book begins with some definitions of psychotherapy and a description of the assumptions on which it rests. Chapter 2 describes the psychotherapist's behavior by defining the basic actions taken by therapists in carrying out verbal psychotherapy.* The student of psychotherapy should be very familiar with them and should have a clear idea of the differences between them, as well as the differences in patients' responses to each. Thus, for instance, both facilitation and confrontation are useful in helping the patient to tell his story and to become aware of his feelings through self-discovery, and they create a different therapy atmosphere than does questioning to accomplish the same aim. Though the patient will give similar information, obtaining it through direct questioning reduces his sense of responsibility for his own feelings. Using confrontation in an empathic way is difficult. Skill in its use requires practice and a clear understanding of what it is. Then, too, many therapists confuse support and reassurance, though each has a different effect on the patient.

Therapists sometimes err in giving the patient too many messages in the same communication. Understanding the differences between the various psychotherapeutic actions and knowing which of them one is using at a given point helps to clarify one's communication, enhancing its therapeutic effect. For these reasons I consider Chapter 2 to be the most important in the book, and the key to making use of the information in subsequent chapters.

Since modern psychotherapy began with analytical work and since most people still think of psychotherapy as being basically insight-oriented, this is the first approach to be discussed, with il-

---

* I am aware that some types of psychotherapy make use of massage and other forms of prolonged or repeated physical contact between patient and therapist. These are not included in this book.

lustrative examples. Then the process-oriented derivatives of psychoanalytic methods are described in Chapter 5. These two approaches, often in combination, are the types of therapy most commonly used in outpatient clinics and private offices, though increasingly the behavior therapy methods described in Chapter 9 are being adopted with voluntary outpatients who have a neurosis.

Supportive psychotherapy, described in Chapter 6, is useful with depressed patients, many of whom are receiving antidepressants, and with patients unable to function socially because of chronic anxiety and depression. It is also the approach most effective with patients who have chronic medical illness.

Crisis intervention, discussed in Chapter 7, is applicable in a broad range of settings, among them mental health clinics, college counseling centers, student mental health services, medical clinics and hospitals, and in outpatient private practice. Social rehabilitation, the subject of Chapter 8, is used primarily in the treatment of chronically psychotic patients and, with variations, that of alcoholics.

A word of warning to the reader is in order here. The application of these methods is not so simple as the case vignettes and excerpts might lead one to believe. For one thing, the patient will always elicit an emotional response from the therapist, of which he may not always be fully aware but which can cloud his judgment or cause him to behave in non-therapeutic ways. And to the degree that the therapist is aware of his emotional response, it may be stressful to him. For these reasons the beginning therapist should always have an opportunity to discuss each session with a supervisor. This provides necessary support for the therapist, and can often help him deal more effectively with his emotional reactions to patients.

Another reason that learning to conduct psychotherapy is difficult is that the beginning student is usually preoccupied with technique (*What should I say now? Is confrontation appropriate here, or should I just listen and wait?*), and this interferes with his attention to the patient as well as with the rapport between them.

This is unavoidable in the early stages of training but, with time and experience, concern over the technical aspects of treatment diminishes and with it some of the tension felt by the student. Even an experienced therapist, however, should continue to scrutinize his response to each patient, and his professional behavior in each session of therapy.

REFERENCES

Bandura, A. "Behavioral Modifications through Modeling Procedures." In Krasner, L., and Ullman, L., *Research in Behavior Modification*. New York: Holt, Rinehart and Winston, 1966.
———. *Social Learning Theory*. Morristown, N.J.: General Learning Press, 1971.
Freud, S. "Remembering, Repeating and Working Through." In *Standard Edition of the Complete Psychological Works of Sigmund Freud*, ed. by J. Strachey, Vol. XII. London: Hogarth Press, 1958.
Kaiser, H. *Effective Psychotherapy*, ed. by L. B. Fierman. New York: Free Press, 1965.
———. "The Problem of Responsibility in Psychotherapy." *Psychiatry* 18:205-211, 1955.

ELEMENTS OF PSYCHOTHERAPY

1

FUNDAMENTAL CONCEPTS
OF PSYCHOTHERAPY

Psychotherapy is one of the few methods of treatment about which disagreement and controversy extend even to the nature of the method itself. This confusion was best characterized in a tongue-in-cheek definition offered by Rainy (1950): "Psychotherapy is an undefined technique applied to unspecified cases with unpredictable results. For this technique, we recommend rigorous training." London (1964) added, "It is easier to practice psychotherapy than to explain it."

Despite this lack of agreement about its fundamental nature, psychotherapy is widely used by a variety of health professionals, particularly psychiatrists, psychologists, social workers, and psychiatric nurses. These professionals practice many kinds of psychotherapy, and the type of therapy cannot be identified by the profession. Though one group of psychotherapists with additional specialized training—the psychoanalysts—are for the most part psychiatrists, psychologists and, with lesser frequency, social workers also become psychoanalysts.

Rainy and London notwithstanding, some useful definitions of psychotherapy have been made. One of the best of these is Jerome Frank's (1963):

Attempts to enhance a person's feeling of well-being are usually labeled treatment, and every society trains some of its members to apply this form of influence. Treatment always involves a personal relationship between healer and sufferer. Certain types of therapy rely primarily on the healer's ability to mobilize healing forces in the sufferer by psychological means. These forms of treatment may be generically termed psychotherapy.

According to Frank, psychotherapy has the following components— in his words:

1. A trained socially sanctioned healer, whose healing powers are accepted by the sufferer and by his social group or an important segment of it.
2. A sufferer who seeks relief from the healer.
3. A circumscribed, more or less structured series of contacts between the healer and the sufferer, through which the healer, often with the aid of a group, tries to produce certain changes in the sufferer's emotional state, attitudes, and behavior.

Maurice Levine, a psychiatrist who was a pioneer in the introduction of psychotherapy into medical care, described it in these terms (1948):

Psychotherapy means therapy by psychological means. . . . it means treatment applied directly to the "mind," by which we mean not to a separate entity, but the functioning of the person as a human being. Psychotherapy includes the direct treatment of one person, as a person, by another. It also includes the indirect treatment of one person by another, through the intermediary of other persons or situations. . . . in general, psychotherapy can be defined as the provision by the physician of new life experiences which can influence a patient in the direction of health.

Defining psychotherapy in more operational terms, Curran and Partridge wrote (1955):

Psychotherapy aims at relieving symptoms of psychic origin by adjusting the attitudes that have led to their development . . . by . . . explanation, suggestion, persuasion, and re-education.

Though at first glance this appears to be a restricted range of behavior for the therapist, the broadest definitions of these four terms encompass most of what psychotherapists do, as will be seen in Chapter 2.

The nature of psychotherapy is further clarified by Ford and Urban (1963):

> Individual verbal psychotherapy appears to have four major elements. First, it involves two people in interaction. The interaction is highly confidential. The patient is required to discuss himself in an intimate fashion. . . . Second, the mode of interaction is usually limited to the verbal realm. . . . Third, the interaction is relatively prolonged. . . . Fourth, this relationship has as its definite and agreed purpose, changes in the behavior of one of the participants.

In summary, they write that "individual verbal psychotherapy is a procedure wherein two persons engage in a prolonged series of emotion-arousing interactions, mediated primarily by verbal exchanges, the purpose of which is to produce changes in the behaviors of one of the pair."

In sum, a psychotherapist may be a member of any of the helping professions, medical or non-medical; may undertake brief or prolonged efforts to improve the state of health or well-being of the patient (or client); and may employ psychotherapy as part of an overall treatment plan, or as the sole method of treatment for a given patient. In Chapter 2 we shall explore the types of communication employed by psychotherapists.

ASSUMPTIONS UNDERLYING PSYCHOTHERAPY

That psychotherapy is effective

Objective evaluations of the outcome of psychotherapy have been few in number and inconclusive in their findings. A problem common to all of them is defining objective measures of success or failure. Eysenck (1966) reviewed all the outcome studies he could find and concluded that the studies did not show that psychother-

apy has a significant effect. It is his contention that neurotic patients treated by psychotherapy improve to the same degree as
similar individuals who do not receive psychotherapy, and that
neurotics tend to improve in time in any event. In the same 1966
symposium on the effects of psychotherapy, J. D. Frank commented that there is much "soft" evidence for acceleration of
improvement through psychotherapy as well as "harder" evidence
for immediate improvement with short-term psychotherapy. The
question of just how effective psychotherapy is remains unanswered,
however. Differences in the objectives of therapy, differences in
conceptions of what psychotherapy is and how long it should last,
and the lack of reliable criteria for evaluating results prevent us
from answering the critics of one or another form of psychotherapy. Many have come to the conclusion that all types of psychotherapy are about equally effective. This suggests the possibility
that features common to them all are the essential therapeutic elements of the process.

That behavior can be changed
Therapists often characterize the changes in their patients' behavior as changes in communication style, life style, interpersonal relations, interpersonal transactions, or character. These are all ways
of describing the type of change a therapist believes to be the outcome of successful psychotherapy. A secondary assumption is that
such changes are more or less permanent, continuing after the therapy has ended.

There is very little evidence to support the claims of schools of
therapy that aim to produce changes of this sort. Nor is it clear
that personality changes during therapy do not merely reflect the
alleviation of anxiety, depression, or phobias. Successful treatment
may lead to an apparent personality change that in fact is only the
emergence of a patient's basic personality traits from paralysis by
fear or depression. It is likely, also, that social learning with consequent personal growth can take place more easily after anxiety or
depression have been reduced.

That insight can cause behavioral change
Two types of insight are commonly discussed: *genetic*, or insight
into the factors presumed to have caused the symptoms; and *dynamic*, or insight into the interactions going on between oneself
and others. Most therapists who set store on these insights believe
that behavioral change occurs when attitudes, feelings, and strivings
that are connected with symptoms and were formerly unconscious
become conscious. Some insight-oriented therapists, however, feel
that insight only facilitates cognitive control of behavior and that
efforts to alter the behavior then must come from the patient.

A corollary assumption not shared by all therapists who believe
that insight is therapeutic is that interpretations by the therapist
can create insight. A minority of therapists who believe in the
value of insight do not accept this assumption. These therapists
tend to believe that insight about oneself occurs when paralyzing
inhibitions, anxiety, or other symptoms disappear, allowing a person to appreciate his impact on others. Still others believe that insight—when it occurs—is a by-product of therapy, and is not at all
necessary for therapy to be helpful.

That psychological or social manipulation
can cause behavior change
Included under this assumption are suggestion, direction, counseling, structuring the environment, and the various techniques of behavior modification.

That interaction with an individual who offers support
and communication can change a person's behavior
All therapists accept some, some accept most, and a few accept all,
of the above assumptions. Obviously, one would have to begin
with one or more of these assumptions to be able to engage in
psychotherapy. Equally obviously, assumptions a psychotherapist
makes will influence his behavior with patients, since:

1. The psychotherapist forms a mental set that influences his perception of the patient. As a patient speaks, the therapist will lis-

ten for those communications that best afford him the opportunity to take the kind of action that he considers therapeutic.
2. Most therapists do not behave in a random way with their patients. While their behavior is a part of the repertoire of normal human social behavior, it is an unusual selection based on the therapist's intent to influence his patient's behavior or emotional state. An insight therapist, for instance, will say things he thinks are likely to create insight. A transactional analyst will talk about the types of transactions that make it possible to use the concepts and terminology of "transactional analysis." A supportive therapist will make statements and behave in ways that express understanding and empathy. A directive therapist will give his patient more specific advice on how to behave. Clearly, the nature of the relation will be strongly influenced by the therapist's view of what is therapeutic.

Goffman (1969) has described the therapist's behavior as "strategic interaction." He defines this as behaving in a way in which one person is assessing the behavior of the other and responding cautiously, rather than openly and spontaneously. Interestingly, Goffman points out that paranoid individuals engage in strategic interactions at all times. This does not mean that psychotherapists are paranoid but that the therapist, in his professional role, shares with the paranoid person a selective response to certain cues from the other person, paying much less attention to information not relevant to his convictions and responding in a careful way.

THE THERAPEUTIC CONTRACT

There is always a contract between the patient, or client, and the therapist. In some forms of therapy this is openly discussed. In other forms it only gradually becomes as apparent to the patient as it is to the therapist. The contract is based on the fact that the patient is a layman seeking help from an expert. There are terms under which he can receive this help. Some of these are fairly instrumental, such as the appointment time, the frequency of the appointments, the fee, the way it will be paid, and so on. Other terms may or may not be discussed, as, for instance, whether certain topics of conversation are more important than others; whether the individual is expected to report certain information or experiences such as dreams; and whether the patient is expected to carry out certain tasks. The contract includes a promise—implied, or sometimes stated—that the therapist will work with the patient in such a way that if the patient carries out his part of the contract, the therapist will do his best to maximize the possibility of improvement. The patient (or client), on the other hand, can terminate the contract at any time and has far less obligation to continue the relation.

Some types of psychotherapy are so closely tied to a specific theory about the cause of behavior disorder or mental illness that the definition of psychotherapy prescribes, to a large extent, the behavior of the therapist. More empirical approaches give the therapist greater freedom of action and more room for spontaneity. A problem arises if a psychotherapist continues to behave as prescribed by his conceptual model when the patient fails to improve, or becomes worse, after a reasonable period of treatment. One reason for this is that the dedicated psychotherapist of any school can usually explain away his failures within the terms of his own theory. However bad for science, this is not necessarily bad for the majority of patients, since therapists themselves undoubtedly need support in the difficult work of changing the behavior of people who are suffering and failing to meet the demands of life. For patients who do not improve with treatment, however, inflexible adherence to a chosen method can actually be harmful.

To the beginning student of psychotherapy, the treatment method seems nebulous and its application very demanding. But there are guidelines, and these will be provided in the chapters to follow. First, the kinds of behavior common to all forms of psychotherapy will be discussed, then the more common types of psychotherapy.

REFERENCES

Curran, D., and Partridge, M. *Psychological Medicine*. London: Livingstone, 1955.

Eysenck, H. J. *The Effects of Psychotherapy*. New York: International Science Press, 1966.

Ford, D. H., and Urban, H. B. *Systems of Psychotherapy*. New York: Wiley, 1963.

Frank, J. D. *Persuasion and Healing*. Baltimore: The Johns Hopkins Press, 1961.

Goffman, E. *Strategic Interaction*. Philadelphia: University of Pennsylvania Press, 1969.

Henry, W. E.; Sims, J. H.; and Spray, S. L. *The Fifth Profession: Becoming a Psychotherapist*. San Francisco: Jossey-Bass, 1971.

Levine, M. *Psychotherapy in Medical Practice*. New York: Macmillan, 1948.

London, P. *The Modes and Morals of Psychotherapy*. New York: Holt, Rinehart and Winston, 1964.

Rainy, V., ed. *Training in Clinical Psychology*. New York: Prentice-Hall, 1950.

2

THE PSYCHOTHERAPIST'S BEHAVIOR

The beginning student of psychotherapy is invariably anxious and uncertain about what is expected of him or her. The question "How should I behave with the patient?" is often asked of instructors and supervisors. While no formula can be given, it is helpful to know that a limited range of behavior is common to psychotherapy and that the characteristic actions of therapists can be described (Adler and Enelow, 1965).

The psychotherapist's behavior usually differs somewhat between the earliest interviews, when data are gathered for selecting therapeutic objectives or an approach to therapy, and later interviews. For this reason, we shall consider first the initial interview.

THE INITIAL INTERVIEW

Whether a patient will undertake therapy with a given psychotherapist is often determined by the skill and sensitivity with which the first interview is conducted. The practitioner's goals for this interview are threefold: data gathering, establishing a therapeutic contract, and beginning the therapeutic relation itself. Although data gathering will go on throughout psychotherapy, its role becomes increasingly subordinate to other goals after the first several interviews. Success in choosing objectives that are appropriate for a given patient depends on the skill with which the therapist gathers data in the initial interview, and to a certain extent in all of the early interviews.

Because of the importance of acquiring information for diagnosis and for choosing a treatment approach, the therapist's focus in the earliest interviews differs from that in later sessions. At the beginning his attention is directed toward cues from observed behavior and from such content of the patient's account as will influence his decision about appropriate goals and strategies. For example, it is important to gauge the patient's ability to stand back and "look at himself," as well as his need for concrete advice. Such characteristics may determine whether an insight-oriented or a directive approach to therapy will be taken.

Characteristics of the patient's style of relating to others, particularly those in authority, will become apparent if the interview is sufficiently open-ended rather than directive and interrogative. This will provide evidence about some of his interpersonal problems, and indicate how he will relate to the therapist as well. Some patients are unsure how to behave and may not easily be able to assume the role of psychotherapy patient because of lack of familiarity with it. This is particularly true of patients from cultures where the psychotherapist who is a health professional is unknown, even though counselors such as ministers, faith healers, or respected elders may be utilized in much the same way as is the psychotherapist in our culture. Information about symptoms, type of thinking (abstract or concrete), disorders of thinking (such as paranoid delusions), and mood will contribute to a diagnostic formulation. This is obviously important, since severe depression or psychosis, for example, suggest different approaches to therapy than might be chosen with a patient suffering from neurosis or a personality problem creating social discomfort. This point will be discussed further in Chapter 3.

During the interview patients naturally behave in different ways depending on their psychological state, and they differ also depending on their socio-economic status and cultural background. Hollingshead and Redlich (1958) discovered that upper and upper-middle class subjects are most likely to receive verbal or insight-oriented therapies, while lower class subjects are most likely to be treated with directive or physical methods (such as drugs or electric shock treatment). A similar correlation was found between the diagnosis and social class. Upper and upper-middle class persons are more likely to be classified as neurotic; lower-middle and lower class persons are diagnosed as psychotic more frequently than those in the upper strata. The studies of Koos (1954) suggest that lower class subjects consider far fewer of their discomforts appropriate for reporting to a physician or other health professional. This correlates with the experience of many psychiatric clinics that patients of lower socio-economic status who come voluntarily for psychotherapy tend to have more serious difficulties than those of middle or upper class origins.

As mentioned above, patients from different cultures behave somewhat differently with psychotherapists. Mexican-Americans, for instance, may consult a faith healer first, rather than a health professional, and may expect specific directions from the therapist (Clark, 1970; Rubel, 1966). Zborowski (1969) found that Americans of New England, Irish, Jewish, and Italian background all behaved differently in the way they described and reacted to pain. Not surprisingly, patients who have previously undergone psychotherapy tend to feel most comfortable in the patient role, and most readily provide the diagnostic data needed in the initial interview. They tend to expect the therapist to use an approach to therapy similar to that which they have already experienced.

Thus, the patient's symptoms, personal attributes, socio-economic status, ethnicity, psychological state, and previous experiences with mental health care will all be factors in the patient's choice of therapist where he has a choice of private practitioner, in the decision as to which therapist to assign to him in a clinic, and in the therapist's choice of a treatment method.

A clear description of the initial data-gathering interview will be found in *Interviewing and Patient Care* (Enelow and Swisher, 1972). Particularly relevant to this discussion are the open-ended interview, and the principle of moving through a cycle of information-seeking behavior that begins with low use of authority and proceeds to more directive queries.

The interview is best begun with a broad, open-ended question such as "What kind of difficulty are you having?" As the patient responds, the therapist should encourage a spontaneously elaborated account through facilitating remarks and gestures. In the early part of the first interview it is much better to look inquiringly, nod, or say "Go on," than to ask specific questions. If the therapist notes that the patient is having difficulty in telling his story, or appears to be too upset to talk, he should point it out in a supportive way, describing the difficulty. Such observations as "You seem to be having difficulty in speaking about this," or "You seem upset," may be very helpful in bringing out the patient's story of his conflicts or uncertainties. Puzzling inconsistencies should be pointed out in a non-threatening way that expresses the therapist's perplexity. Direct questions should be used later in the interview to fill in gaps. They should not interrupt the patient's account or change its direction.

The principle is this: *Spontaneous reporting tends to produce the broadest range of information, both verbal and non-verbal.* When verbal communication ceases, non-verbal communication continues. Describing his non-verbal behavior encourages the patient to express his inner experience. All this increases the likelihood that the patient will accept a responsible role in the course of therapy. At this stage, direct questions are given a lesser role (though used later in the interview), as they tend to encourage passivity and lead the patient to wait for direction from the therapist.

Encouraging free expression of feelings by the patient, in a supportive atmosphere where he feels it is safe to express himself, makes for early development of trust in the therapist—an important element in all psychotherapy. Patients often discontinue treatment quite early unless they feel that they can talk to the therapist and that he will listen and try to understand. Unless the patient can achieve some degree of trust and confidence, a therapeutic contract as described in Chapter 1 cannot be established. This supportive data gathering need not be limited to a single interview but should be continued until the therapist is prepared to choose a therapeutic approach.

Certain aspects of the therapeutic contract should be made explicit at once, or at least as soon as the therapist is certain about them. These include frequency of visits, fee, and other requirements that the therapist may make of the patient. If certain behavior is prescribed by the therapist, such as keeping a journal, or disclosing all thoughts during therapy sessions, or doing relaxation exercises at home, this should be described to the patient as soon as possible. In discussing these details, however, the therapist must move only as fast as the patient can follow, and avoid using the jargon of the profession.

Since all psychotherapy depends to some extent on the support inherent in the relationship, regardless of the ultimate goals of a given treatment course, a therapist who fails to be perceived by the patient as supportive in the initial interview will probably not have that patient in treatment very long.

PSYCHOTHERAPY BEHAVIOR*

Facilitation
Actions intended by the therapist to call forth or encourage communication but do not specify what type of response is expected, and usually do not obligate the patient to respond, are called *facilitation*. Among examples are encouraging sounds and facial expressions, as well as signs of recognition, interest, or receptiveness,

---

* The definitions in this section of the chapter were formulated in the course of research on psychotherapy and interviewing done in collaboration with Leta McKinney Adler, Ph.D., during the years 1961–1968.

such as leaning forward. It is facilitating to show attention by nodding the head or saying things like "I see" and "Yes." A puzzled look may also have a facilitating effect. Facilitation is an important aspect of psychotherapy. Often it takes place without the awareness of the therapist, but it is the essence of active listening. Facilitation can be pushed too far, however. Exaggerated gestures, facial expressions, or utterances may be perceived as ungenuine and thus create distrust. Ungenuine behavior on the therapist's part does not help establish a therapeutic relation.

Support
Any action by the therapist that communicates his interest in, liking for, or understanding of the patient, promoting a feeling of security in the relationship, represents *support*. This begins with a smile as the patient enters the room, or some friendly sign of recognition such as a greeting, a handshake, or placing a hand on the shoulder. It can continue with questions like "How are you?" or "Did you have a nice holiday?" Any gesture of cordiality is supportive. Genial comments about the weather, or similar brief comments about other matters unrelated to the therapy and suggesting that the relation has a social dimension beyond the mere extending of treatment services, are supportive, though they may not be appropriate in forms of therapy such as psychoanalysis. Similarly, using the patient's first name or nickname is supportive—if inappropriate for some types of therapy. The same can be said of expressions of approval for something the patient has just said or done. Support can be expressed by a warm smile and a nod in which the non-verbal communication is "I understand." The expression of empathy, "I can understand how you feel," might be described as the paradigm of support.

Verbal expressions of support in the absence of a supportive attitude, will, however, fail in their purpose. A supportive attitude is compounded of a number of elements (Enelow and Wexler, 1966): (1) genuine interest in and concern for the patient; (2) a feeling of warmth or friendliness toward the patient; (3) a desire to be of help; and (4) maintenance of sufficient reserve that the therapist remains clearly aware that he is engaging in a helping relation and preserves his own personal and professional identity. It is probably impossible to be supportive toward a patient one dislikes. The supportive attitude will be discussed further in Chapter 6.

Confrontation

When a psychotherapist says something with the intent of making the patient aware of an aspect of his behavior which the therapist observed, he is using *confrontation*. This is usually achieved with a description of the patient's appearance and behavior during the interview and often involves low levels of inference about the patient's tone of voice or non-verbal communication, as in the following examples: "You said that in a way that gave me the impression you were asking me for my opinion about it." "I noticed that though you were describing something very troublesome, you looked quite cheerful." "It's interesting that the expression around your eyes does not change when you smile with your mouth." "You look very angry."

A therapist may also confront his patient with a statement about the content of their communication, particularly if there is a dominant theme. For example, "Everything you tell me has one theme—how nobody understands you." Or, "I find it puzzling that you say you have no friends, when you have mentioned a lot of people that you see very often." Confrontations used early in therapy tend to be rather simple, such as, "You look angry," or "You look depressed." As the therapy proceeds, if confrontation is an important part of it, the therapist's statements become more complex and deal with content and discrepancies in what the patient is saying.

Confrontations should be used sparingly, and without implying disapproval of the behavior involved. They are simply a way of drawing a patient's attention toward his own words or behavior. If used too often, they can develop a nagging quality.

Reassurance

All behavior of the therapist (especially his utterances) that tends
to restore the patient's sense of well-being, worthiness, or confidence in himself has the function of *reassurance*. Expressions of
optimism about a good outcome of therapy or other matters of
concern to the patient give reassurance. Observations that help restore the patient's faith in his own abilities, skills, intelligence, or
capacity to cope with difficulties are reassuring, as are those that
help restore faith in family members, doctors, or others of importance to him.

As with support, the therapist's attitude is crucial in giving reassurance. Reassuring words without genuine optimism based on
realistic expectations are not likely to be effective, at least not for
very long.

Suggestion

Suggestion involves giving advice or guidance in a manner that
does not require compliance and does not imply a loss of the patient's autonomy. Concrete ways of attaining a desired goal may
be proposed without directing the patient to carry them out. Certain questions represent suggestions, as for example, "Have you
thought about the effect on your wife, if you do that?"—which
suggests caution before taking a given action. Expressions of strong
approval, as used in the reinforcement procedures of behavior modification, are suggestions—i.e., that such behavior be repeated. Conversely, to ignore or mildly disapprove of behavior as in negative
reinforcement or extinction is also to make a suggestion. A common form of suggestion in psychotherapy is to express a general
opinion about the type of situation in which the patient finds himself. For example: "It is better to take a stand than to feel unhappy because you permit others to do things of which you disapprove." Or, "If you don't tell people how you really feel about
their behavior, they will have no way of knowing that you disapprove."

Sometimes suggestion is carried out by proposing two alternatives, one clearly less desirable than the other, as for example, "You can go on suffering as you are, or do something about your situation and move out of the house." Discussions of the use of suggestion will appear in the sections on supportive therapy, crisis intervention, social rehabilitation, and elsewhere in this book. Suggestion is used much more often than is commonly supposed or recognized by the therapists themselves.

Direction

Telling the patient what to do is *direction*. When a therapist attempts to control or supervise the patient in a way that does not recognize or greatly limits his freedom of choice he is being directive. Therapists give direction about standards of conduct, decisions about what a patient should do and what to avoid, and the course of action that must be followed if therapy is to continue. Direction plays an important part in some types of therapy, including crisis intervention, social rehabilitation, and behavior modification. In other types, especially the insight-oriented and process-oriented, it is expressly avoided.

Questioning

Questions may be phrased either with great specificity, limiting the response, or as suggestions, in which case they are rather open-ended and allow the patient much leeway in answering. Patients respond to open-ended questions with more spontaneity and feel free to say more than when questions are straightforwardly interrogatory. A directive question usually seeks a specific piece of information and thus restricts the range of the patient's response.

Although some therapists tend to use questions for their facilitating effect, this can result in structuring the relation into an active therapist-passive patient process in which the patient waits for questions before communicating anything. Questions are probably best used for clarification rather than for facilitation.

Interpretation

When a therapist makes a statement about the patient based on an inference that links events—either causally or by analogy—or that ascribes to the patient a motive or emotional state, he is making an *interpretation*. There are various levels of inference in interpretations, and most confrontations make some degree of inference, so that the line between interpretation and confrontation is blurred. On the whole, though, the degree to which a statement is based on a directly observable behavior rather than on an inference determines whether it is a confrontation (which leaves the evaluation or explanation up to the patient) or an interpretation (which presents the patient with some kind of explanation).

Interpretations at a low level of inference often deal more with the therapeutic process than with the content of what the patient says—i.e., "You act as though you wanted to make sure that I do exactly what you want me to." There is greater inference in a statement like, "You treat me as you do all other men [women] in a way that puts them all in the role of being your father [mother]." Inferences at a high level are usually based as much on theory as on observation, as an interpretation dealing with the oedipus complex would be.

Some interpretations deal with the here-and-now: "You aren't saying anything today because you are angry with me." Others deal with the there-and-then: "You hated your father because he came between you and your mother." Interpretations that deal with the patient's present motivations are sometimes called *dynamic*. Those that deal with causative influences from the past presumed to underlie the patient's present behavior are sometimes called *genetic*. Those that deal with the interaction itself are called *process interpretations*. In psychoanalysis, process interpretations often have a genetic aspect and are called *transference interpretations*; that is, the therapist-patient relation is interpreted as a re-enactment of an early significant relation. In general, dynamic and process interpretations (with the exception of the transference type) have a lower level of inference than genetic interpretations.

ADDITIONAL DESCRIPTIONS OF THERAPIST'S BEHAVIOR
Advice and guidance
Advice and guidance are often given to patients who have more or
less specific situational problems, or who seem to be functioning
at such a primitive psychological level that they cannot make essential everyday decisions. Advice and guidance are a mixture of
support, suggestion, and direction, as defined above.

Silence
Silence is often very useful in helping patients to communicate. It
can be supportive, it can be facilitative, and at times it can carry an
implicit direction—as when a patient asks a question and the therapist is silent, in effect saying "Keep on talking." Thus, the context and the therapist's attitude will define what a silence means to
the patient. This will be discussed in several later chapters.

When a patient is silent, this often poses a severe trial of pa-
tience for the therapist; inexperienced therapists, in particular, are
uncomfortable with the silent patient. Yet very often the best way
to deal with silence is to examine the non-verbal communication
rather than to be concerned about why the patient is not talking.
In other words, it is really not necessary that someone be talking at
all times during the session. Some patients are silent much of the
time, even though they continue in therapy. Such patients are extremely difficult to treat and are probably best treated with process-
oriented therapy (Enelow, 1960).

Reinforcement and behavior modification
Reinforcement is a part of all psychotherapy. Whether the therapist is aware of it or not, he is indicating by his behavior that he
values some of the patient's activities, statements, or decisions
more than others. Some types of therapy, however, rely on reinforcement and negative reinforcement as the principal methods of
treatment. In such therapy, attempts are made to reinforce desired

behavior through suggestion, direction, and carefully worked out reinforcement schedules; and this is the chief activity of the therapist. Even in behavior therapy, however, there must be an element of support if the patient is to have enough faith in the therapist to continue the therapy.

Modeling

Bandura (1960) points out that one of the fundamental means by which new modes of behavior are acquired and existing patterns are modified is modeling—that is, observing and emulating the performance of models. In psychotherapy it is the therapist's behavior that serves as the model for the patient. When a given behavior has been "modeled" by the therapist, if it is appropriate for the patient and is followed by positive reinforcement (praise, support, and so on) of the patient's imitative efforts, it is likely to be repeated. Subsequent attempts by the patient to carry out such behavior in the real world may be further reinforced by positive results (or a failure of the feared consequences to occur, as in phobias). Although modeling probably enters into all psychotherapy, it is a planned part of some behavior therapies (see Chapter 9).

REFERENCES

Adler, L. M., and Enelow, A. J. "Manual for the Use of the PIA Scale." Mimeographed. Department of Psychiatry, University of Southern California, 1965.
Bandura, A. *Principles of Behavior Modification.* New York: Holt, Rinehart and Winston, 1969.
Clark, M. *Health in the Mexican-American Culture.* Los Angeles and Berkeley: University of California Press, 1970.
Enelow, A. J. "The Silent Patient." *Psychiatry* 23:153–58, 1960.
Enelow, A. J., and Swisher, S. N. *Interviewing and Patient Care.* New York: Oxford University Press, 1972.
Enelow, A. J., and Wexler, M. *Psychiatry in the Practice of Medicine.* New York: Oxford University Press, 1966.
Hollingshead, A. B., and Redlich, F. C. *Social Class and Mental Illness.* New York: Wiley, 1958.

Koos, E. L. *The Health of Regionville*. New York: Columbia University Press, 1954.
Rubel, A. J. *Across the Tracks*. Austin: University of Texas Press, 1966.
Zborowski, M. *People in Pain*. San Francisco: Jossey-Bass, 1969.

3

CHOOSING GOALS AND OBJECTIVES
FOR PSYCHOTHERAPY

After one or more initial data-gathering interviews, the therapist usually decides how to proceed with a given patient. Some believe that "procedures" are antithetical to the concept of psychotherapy as a human interaction (Fierman, 1975). But without specified goals, treatment tends to become protracted, if not endless. The therapist is well-advised to attempt to be realistic about what can be accomplished, in approximately what period of time and at what expense. Setting goals helps to keep both patient and therapist from settling into a comfortably ambiguous relation that may go on indefinitely. A frank discussion of goals, and approximate time and expense of treatment, can help to prevent forced terminations because of economic or other external considerations without regard to improvement in the patient's emotional or behavioral problems.

There appear to be three general positions among schools of psychotherapy as to who sets the goals for psychotherapy (Ford and Urban, 1963). Psychoanalysts and many behavior therapists believe that the therapist is an expert whose task it is to determine what the problem is and what the remedy should be. Therapists who work with severely psychotic patients also tend to hold this view. The opposite viewpoint, held by process-oriented psychotherapists, is that the patient must decide the goals of treatment. Some therapists go farther and claim that only the patient can know when therapy has accomplished its objectives. The third position—somewhere between the other two and probably the one most widely held—is that therapist and patient should decide together on some goals toward which they both can work. In this view the therapist has responsibility for the diagnosis and for proposing goals to the patient for discussion. Agreement about what they will try to accomplish—an important part of establishing the therapeutic contract—is seen by many therapists as the first task in any course of psychotherapy, once a diagnosis has been made and a psychotherapy approach has been chosen by the therapist.

Often the objectives will include the modification or elimination of disordered responses and the development of new and more rewarding behavior. In some cases the objective may be to acquire tolerance for one's existing behavior patterns. The approach to achieving each type of goal varies with the therapist's viewpoint. Some rely on insight, others advocate learning new behavior patterns without regard for whether the patient develops insight about himself and the origin of his problems. The average therapist who is not wedded to a single model of psychotherapy attempts to be flexible, and modifies his approach according to the characteristics of each patient. More and more, therapists are heeding Barten's plea for "therapeutic parsimony" (1971) and are likely to try simple or briefer procedures before committing themselves to more complex or time-consuming ones.

R.C., a 47-year-old employee of a small business, consulted a psychiatrist because of a fear that he might commit suicide. During the initial interview there emerged the story of a man who had suffered intermittent emotional deprivations early in life, and had few opportunities to make friends during his pre-adolescent years. He had become better at making friends, had married and was the father of three children. After the age of 40, however, with increasing intensity he felt lonely, somewhat depressed and pre-

occupied with his early experiences. He began to think about suicide. Toward the close of the interview, he said, "What I really
want is to feel less alone. I want to live in the present, and stop
dwelling on the past." He had stated the goal, one to which the
therapist could agree.

Not all patients are able to take part in a responsible way in
choosing the goals of their treatment. To the patient with a psychotic disorder who accepts treatment because of pressure from society or his immediate family, the goals set by the therapist may
have little or no meaning, at least at the outset. In such instances,
the goals of therapy are shaped to a large extent by the diagnosis
but are influenced also by constraints such as time, money, and
other circumstances over which the patient has little or no control. Yet it is often a goal of treatment to reach a point where the
patient can understand and take part in setting further goals.

Most therapists agree that a patient must be suffering, unhappy,
subject to anxiety, or dissatisfied with at least some aspects of his
behavior in order for therapy to take place. Most would agree also
that the goals of treatment must in some way be related to the nature of this unhappiness, suffering, or dissatisfaction.

Therapeutic goals should be realistic and, at the very least, acceptable to the patient as well as the therapist. Most therapists
would also add that they must be potentially attainable within reasonable time limits. These three characteristics may seem to be
self-evident. Unfortunately, far too many courses of therapy are begun with highly unrealistic ideas about what a patient will agree to
do or what can be accomplished. Not infrequently, therapists set
unrealistic goals such as changing a person's basic temperament
without regard for the complaints articulated by the patient.

The psychotherapy approaches, or types of psychotherapy style,
to be discussed in subsequent chapters are usually chosen for somewhat different though overlapping groups of patients. Their goals
may be grouped in these major categories: crisis intervention, insight, symptom relief, and social rehabilitation.

Crisis intervention

Crisis intervention is based on the work of Lindemann (1944), who observed that in a situation of social and emotional crisis individuals become disturbed, regress, and develop symptoms of anxiety or depression. He resolved the crisis by giving them the opportunity to express their feelings in reaction to the acutely stressful situation or event. The patients in crisis were encouraged to talk about it to an interested person who offered support, appropriate reassurance where necessary, and counseling about specific actions they might take in order to restore stability to their lives.

In crisis intervention it is assumed that most people, even though they may have some neurotic symptoms or chronic life problems, can function at a reasonably effective level most of the time, but that if they encounter a crisis with which they are unable to cope, they will regress or become anxious or depressed. Helping them through the crisis by encouraging the expression of feelings and giving support and counseling should return them to their pre-crisis adjustment state. Attempts to go beyond resolving the reaction to the crisis are not considered to be part of crisis intervention. This is a useful approach with individuals who have indeed functioned reasonably effectively until a crisis occurred. The choice of this type of therapy has less to do with a diagnosis assigned to the patient than with the circumstances under which symptoms appeared. Often no attempt is made to assign a diagnosis.

The concept of crisis intervention is sometimes extended beyond its original definition. Some patients who are chronically psychotic or in other ways severely disturbed have periods of acute exacerbation with symptoms of even greater severity. The term *crisis intervention* is sometimes applied to efforts to deal with these episodes by giving the patients supportive counseling and increased or altered medications. At such times certain patients may be given drug treatment for the first time, or a discontinued drug regimen may be re-instituted. As soon as the acute exacerbation has subsided, the counseling efforts are discontinued, though follow-up medication checks may be continued.

In this application of crisis intervention it is assumed that the level of psychotic disturbance before the crisis is acceptable to the patient and to those around him, and is about the best that can be hoped for with that patient. Once the patient regains that level, it is considered pointless to attempt to achieve more ambitious goals. Patients who are in an on-going psychotherapy and suffer a crisis may be treated with some of the measures used in crisis intervention for the necessary period of time, after which the previous approach may be resumed.

In crisis intervention the goal should be explicitly stated to the patient. The term is not used, of course, but the plan for a time-limited relation to help the patient through the crisis period should be described.

> M.J., a 26-year-old married architectural draftsman, was referred to the psychiatric clinic from the medical clinic. "Since I was fired, I've had these stomach cramps," he said. The initial interview brought out a history of a careful, hardworking, conscientious young man who could not tolerate feelings of failure. When working and feeling productive, he had few or no symptoms. But if told a drawing he had done was unsatisfactory, he would become upset and have stomach pains. When his job was lost in a general cutback, he became upset, had great difficulty telling his wife about it, and developed severe abdominal cramps with diarrhea. After medical evaluation indicated no organic pathology, he was referred for psychotherapy. During the initial interview it became evident that he was not an introspective person and was dissatisfied not with himself but with those around him. At the conclusion of the interview the therapist said, "I don't really feel that you have serious psychological problems. I'll see you a few times and help you deal with this upset and your feelings about losing the job. It shouldn't be more than a few sessions." The patient assented. After four sessions, he felt better and had located another drafting job. Therapy was concluded by mutual agreement.

In this case the patient's goals for himself did not include a wish to alter his inability to tolerate a sense of failure. To attempt to induce the insight that would precede his adoption of such an objec-

tive would have been time-consuming and expensive as well as un-
likely to succeed.

Insight

Insight-oriented types of therapy proceed from the assumption that
patients can be helped by means of a better understanding of
themselves. These approaches can all be traced to Freud's methods of psychoanalysis, even though many now deviate markedly
from them. Insight therapies, in contrast to crisis intervention, de-
emphasize alleviation of the patient's complaints, viewing them as
symptoms of an underlying psychological disorder. In effect, the
symptom serves as one of the motivations to seek treatment for
the underlying disorder. When patients do, in fact, believe this
(i.e., "There must be something really wrong with me or I wouldn't
get into this kind of difficulty") they are usually receptive to the
goal of increased self-knowledge. Because a patient must express
himself openly in this process, it requires a fairly high degree of motivation, a desire to talk, some belief that self-knowledge will be
helpful, at least average intelligence, and the ability to relinquish a
certain amount of defensiveness, accept "criticism," and examine
one's own role in various interactions.

Insight therapies operate at different levels. Some of them aim
to uncover unconscious impulses and tendencies as well as long-
forgotten memories. Others aim for a transactional type of insight
about one's impact on others: these are the process-oriented therapies. Still others deal with motives or tendencies that are not far
from awareness, or of which the patient is dimly aware but the significance of which he fails to grasp. The therapies that aim for one
or another type of insight will be discussed in Chapters 4 and 5.

The insight- and process-oriented therapies are most commonly
chosen for patients with neuroses or milder personality disorders,
rarely for psychotic patients or those with the severe personality
disorders associated with disruptive social behavior. It is sometimes
used successfully in psychosomatic illness. Psychoanalysis, the most

thorough-going and intensive form of insight-oriented therapy, is used almost exclusively in treating neuroses.

Symptom relief

Symptom relief is, of course, the goal of crisis intervention. But there may be situations in which a chronic disorder is best handled by direct attempts to relieve symptoms through behavior therapy techniques, or support and reassurance, or direct advice, or medication. In the severe psychotic disorders, symptom relief is almost always the goal of therapy. And in other situations as well, symptom relief may appropriately be selected as the treatment objective.

The removal of some symptoms by behavior modification may not require an understanding of their genesis. The symptom is extinguished, and the question of why it developed is never addressed. If a symptom is clear-cut and does not accompany a general disorder of social behavior, this may be a simple and expedient therapy approach. For patients who are not introspective or psychologically minded, this approach may succeed where an insight approach would not.

In other cases it is not feasible to undertake therapy that involves an exploration of the patient's relationships or his adaptive behavior. This may be because of the patient's general lack of awareness or sensitivity to these issues. It may be that he has limited intellectual capacity or an organic deficit that interferes with his comprehension. Or it may be that the culture from which the patient comes is one where all professionals are seen as authorities of high status who give advice or directions. In such cases the therapist may choose to make direct efforts to correct the patient's symptoms or maladaptive behavior patterns by giving advice, by persuasion and exhortation, or by using techniques such as relaxation exercises.

When simple direct relief of symptoms is sought, drugs are often prescribed, particularly minor tranquilizers and anti-depressants. In the treatment of depressions, for example, anti-depressant medication plus support may suffice to relieve or eliminate the symptoms.

During the early data-gathering interviews, and especially when the patient is seen with other members of his family, it may become apparent that some external circumstance is producing stress or igniting old conflicts. If this is happening, it may be best to intervene directly with counseling, exploring alternative courses of action, and focusing directly on the circumstances that seem to be creating the problem so as to work toward changing it. If the problem can be resolved, the symptoms should subside or disappear, and in many cases this is a good time to stop the treatment. In a sense, this approach is a variant of crisis intervention used with families and directed at what is often a chronic life circumstance. It aims for improvement in the patient's internal state through external change.

Social rehabilitation
For many chronic psychotic patients, whether in after-care clinics, drug treatment centers, or community mental health programs viewed as alternatives to hospitalization, social rehabilitation is the main therapeutic goal. A common problem is to help patients who have adapted to institutional life learn to function once again in a non-institutional social setting. Through counseling and learning of new skills that may make them employable, patients may begin to develop enough confidence in themselves (with consequent reduction in their agitation or bizarre behavior) to become self-supporting. Others can learn no more than the everyday tasks of non-institutional life such as taking a bus, purchasing groceries, and preparing food. Social rehabilitation is usually accomplished best in groups rather than in individual therapy, although a person (whether a therapist or someone else) with whom the patient has a steady and reliable one-to-one relationship can be very helpful in this process.

REFERENCES

Barten, H. H., ed. *Brief Therapies.* New York: Behavioral Publications, 1971.

Ford, D. H., and Urban, H. B. *Systems of Psychotherapy.* New York:
    Wiley, 1963.
Kaiser, H. *Effective Psychotherapy,* ed. by L. B. Fierman. New York:
    Free Press, 1965.
Lindemann, E. "Symptomatology and Management of Acute Grief."
    American Journal of Psychiatry 101:141–48, 1944.

4

INSIGHT-ORIENTED PSYCHOTHERAPY

The insight-oriented therapies derive from the psychoanalytic method of Sigmund Freud (1856–1939), as do almost all modern systems of psychotherapy except behavior therapy. The concepts of insight as therapeutic and of the influence of unconscious psychological factors on behavior were introduced by Freud. Psychoanalysis, the first insight-oriented treatment method, is not widely used today; yet its influence is seen in the insight- and process-oriented methods that are in general use in the therapy of outpatients who voluntarily seek help.

In the last decade of the nineteenth century, Freud began treating patients suffering from hysteria, in collaboration with Joseph Breuer, a Vienna internist. They called their approach a "cathartic method." By means of hypnosis, they encouraged the expression of fears, conflicts, forgotten traumatic experiences and hitherto unexpressed emotions. After the publication of *Studies on Hysteria* (1895), Breuer withdrew from the collaboration. Freud continued for the remainder of his long career, developing not only a method of treatment but also a complex set of theories concerning human behavior, personality development, psychopathology, and the causes of psychological symptoms.

Freud ceased using hypnosis quite early in his investigations. He found that he could get the information he sought by directing patients to tell everything that came to mind. He called this "free association." In Freud's view at that time, the task of the therapist was to uncover forgotten or repressed memories, many of which were connected with conflicts, the awareness of which the patient could not tolerate and which the patient could not resolve. These buried memories were presumed to sustain the symptoms. In his earlier approaches to treatment, Freud felt that bringing such memories to awareness would cause the symptoms to disappear. Thus his earliest approach to therapy was concerned with the forgotten or buried content of the patient's thoughts and memories. He was particularly concerned with uncovering this content in a way that would also promote the experiencing and expressing of the feelings associated with it.

Freud's further studies made him increasingly aware that recovering forgotten memories and the apparent associated insight were not predictably accompanied by improvement. Gradually he developed new concepts to describe the complexity of the therapeutic task. The first of these was *resistance*.

Freud's early psychoanalytic patients promised to tell everything that occurred to them but soon found that they were unable or unwilling to tell certain things. Sometimes they could think of nothing to say. Freud termed this behavior *resistance* and postulated the phenomenon of defense, a psychological force that prevents the forgotten content from emerging into awareness. He proposed that this was the same force that had created the symptom originally, when the patient repressed a tendency or impulse he considered dangerous or unacceptable to him. The task of the analyst then became one of pointing out or interpreting the resistance. This evolved into a procedure of bringing the resistance itself into awareness as a means of recovering the buried or repressed content.

The second concept was *transference*. Patients behaved toward

Freud in ways that often seemed to reflect feelings associated with their problems. They attributed to him attitudes that reflected their own fears or wishes. He came to consider these responses as having been transferred from feelings once held toward significant persons in their early development. Thus he defined transference as the development of feelings and attitudes toward the therapist which represented revivals of feelings and attitudes toward people of importance in the patient's early, formative years. This became another focus for the psychoanalytic therapist: the unraveling or analysis of the memories and feelings connected with the significant events of those early years as reflected in the patient's behavior with the analyst.

As psychoanalysis evolved, the task of the therapist began to center more and more on transference and resistance. The analyst's primary tool was interpretation. With interpretations the analyst attempted to make the resistance and transference behavior clear to the patient. This would lead to the recovery of the repressed conflicts, fears, and other emotions connected with the forgotten, significant events that were considered to be the causative factors in the neurosis. As Freud described this technique in 1914,

> Finally there was evolved the consistent technique used today, in which the analyst gives up the attempt to bring a particular moment or problem into focus. He contents himself with studying whatever is present for the time being on the surface of the patient's mind, and he employs the art of interpretation mainly for the purpose of recognizing the resistances which appear there, and making them conscious to the patient. (1958)

Later, however, interpretation was used more sparingly, since its frequent use appeared to foster resistance or to provoke more anxiety than the patient could tolerate. The concept of "working through" was added as it became apparent that a single exposure, or "accession to awareness," of unconscious tendencies was insufficient to eliminate symptoms or alter behavior. "Working through" is the term used for repeated re-examination of what are presumed to be unconscious determinants of a patient's behavior and the ways they are expressed. This is a long and arduous task.

The insight-oriented therapies now in use are derivatives of psychoanalysis. Some of them began with students of Freud who left his circle of followers to establish "schools" of their own. Some short-term varieties have been developed by analysts who also taught and practiced classical psychoanalysis. Alexander (1946), for example, advocated wider use of a short-term derivative of psychoanalysis in which an effort is made to produce a "corrective emotional experience" by promoting the re-experiencing of past relationships that were unsatisfactory or troublesome in the new setting of the therapist-patient interaction. Psychoanalysis aims for a painstakingly detailed exploration of the patient's feelings, attitudes, behavior, and relationships, both past and present. The briefer insight-oriented therapies are more focused, more limited in their goals; and they employ interpretation more for clarifying troublesome aspects of the patient's life than for uncovering deeply buried memories with their associated feelings (Stein, 1963; Stewart, 1975).

CHOOSING THE APPROPRIATE PATIENT
FOR INSIGHT-AIMING PSYCHOTHERAPY

There are certain requirements for a patient who is entering insight therapy. Some are attributes of the patient, others relate more to the type of interaction with the therapist. In general, patients are chosen who have average or above-average intelligence, who do not have psychotic symptoms, and who voluntarily seek treatment. As Hollingshead and Redlich (1958) have written, for insight-aiming therapy a cooperative attitude on the part of the patient is essential. They go on to say that a voluntary effort on the part of the patient to understand his troubles and conflicts, a desire to change and a willingness to talk about his problems before choosing a course of action are required. Many authors emphasize the importance of cooperativeness in insight therapy. Hollingshead and Redlich state that "we are not sure what attributes a good patient must have, but they include sensitivity, intelligence, social and intellectual standards similar to the psychiatrist's, a will to do one's best, a desire to improve one's personality and status in life, youth, attractiveness, and charm."

Insight therapists use interpretations to "explain" behavior. Since these are sometimes unpalatable or upsetting, a positive or warm relationship between patient and psychotherapist is required. If the feeling is positive, therapy is most likely to continue despite interpretations that present an unattractive aspect of the patient's personality and are difficult for him to accept.

The types of problems usually treated with insight-oriented therapy are listed in Chapter 3. In general, it is used with patients who have a good prognosis.

LEVELS OF INTERPRETATION

Having determined that an insight-aiming approach is appropriate and that the patient meets the requirements, the therapist must next ask: What level of interpretation should be used? Psychoanalysis, the insight approach with the most ambitious goals, employs interpretations of past conflicts and unconscious motives in addition to interpretations of current behavior, since the method requires that they be reconstructed or remembered and their sequelae in present-day behavior, thought, and emotion made explicit. Other approaches try to clarify the half-hidden, dimly perceived attitudes and feelings of the present that are leading to problems in behavior and interpersonal relations, in the belief that such insight is sufficient for good therapeutic results. This is a more modest goal. It calls for therapy that is usually more focused and of briefer duration than psychoanalysis. Therapist and patient examine current problems, looking to the past only to clarify present-day difficulties. In a more extensive exploration of the past and the present, interpretations tend to involve a higher level of inference. Special training and much practice under supervision are required for this approach.

The following case illustrates a therapy oriented toward examination of current problems.

C.R., a 35-year-old accountant, was referred for psychotherapy by his family physician because of depression of moderate intensity characterized by indecision, feelings of failure, sleeplessness, loss of sexual drive, and a constant "heavy" feeling in his upper abdomen. He had been a moderately successful man, working for a small accounting firm that did "the books" for even smaller businesses. One of these businesses became somewhat more successful, and since he had audited their books for several years and had prepared their tax returns, they offered him a position as Controller of the company. He was elated at first and began his new position with a feeling of great optimism. He moved quickly to establish an accounting, billing, and collection system but in so doing antagonized some of the older executives. One of these men called him in on one occasion and criticized him rather harshly for his aggressive behavior. Soon after, C.R. became depressed, had increasing difficulty in working and began to lose his subordinates. One of these, before leaving for another job, informed C.R. that he could no longer work with him because of his indecisiveness and procrastination. This was an even greater blow, and though C.R. recognized that he had become indecisive and hated to address himself to new tasks since he had become so depressed, he felt that the confrontation was like "kicking a man when he is down." Soon after, he saw his physician to find out whether he could get relief from his distress, and was referred for psychotherapy.

Mr. R. was relatively verbal and able to discuss his symptoms and his recent difficulties. He had not, he said, had depressions or other severe symptoms in the past. Except for an unsatisfying marriage with relatively little communication with his wife and children, he had been fairly successful, though never outstanding, in everything he had attempted. Because he was still functioning reasonably well, going to work every day and doing enough so that his job was not yet in jeopardy, and because he was apparently anxious to talk about his situation, the therapist decided not to use medication and to undertake psychotherapy. Toward the close of the first session the following interchange took place.

PATIENT: Do you think there's any help for me?

THERAPIST: Oh yes, I think so. There are no guarantees, of course, but I think there's a reasonably good chance that psychotherapy can help you.

PATIENT: I want to understand what happened to me. I was an active man, liked my work, felt I was getting somewhere just a year ago. And look at me now. What happened? How did I get this way?

THERAPIST: Well, I really can't say—especially since I saw you for the first time less than an hour ago.

PATIENT: I suppose I have to tell you a lot more. When you find out, will you tell me?

THERAPIST: That's not really how this works. Perhaps it would be most accurate to say that we'll probably both find out.

PATIENT: Yes, I think I see what you mean. O.K. What do I have to do?

THERAPIST: Well, I'd like to see you once a week, for about forty-five or fifty minutes—and I'd like to hear about anything you want to tell me.

PATIENT: You mean, like my life history?

THERAPIST: Or anything else you want to talk about. But I'm as interested in what's going on presently as I am in your past.

PATIENT: How long will I have to come here?

THERAPIST: That's more or less up to you, of course, but I would expect that somewhere between six and twelve or fifteen months ought to be sufficient for you to be able to get over this depression and be able to work again.

PATIENT: That sounds all right. I sure hope it doesn't take fifteen months, though.

Following this, there was a discussion of the fee, and an appointment time was set.

In the next interview, C.R. filled in his life history, rather sketchily. He was the older of two children, having a younger sister. His mother was somewhat self-effacing, relatively inarticulate, and unable to communicate with either the patient or his father. His father was a perfectionist, somewhat autocratic businessman who demanded a very high performance in every area from his son, though he was much less demanding of his daughter. The patient made respectable but not outstanding grades, had some interest in athletics, but applied himself particularly in those areas that related to accounting. Soon after graduating from college he entered an accounting firm, worked hard, and soon was making a rather good income. When he was offered the position of Controller of a newly expanding business, he saw it as his first real "break" and a chance to achieve real success in business. The confrontation with the older executive was a great blow that made him lose confidence in himself.

At this point in his narrative the following interchange took place.

> PATIENT: It seems to have started right there. He accused me of being an ambitious, aggressive young man who didn't have any sensitivity to people's needs. He told me that doing the books for the company was just about my level of ability and to try to work with people as part of an organization was beyond my capabilities. But it wasn't just what he said. There was such a tone of contempt in his voice that I felt like he was dismissing me and everything I'd done as just second-rate or worse.
>
> THERAPIST: Sounds like that really hurt.
>
> PATIENT: That's putting it mildly. I felt shattered.
>
> THERAPIST: You must expect a very high standard of performance from yourself—nothing second-rate.
>
> PATIENT: There's never been a question in my mind about that. *I* expect it—it's always been expected *of* me.

He then went on at length and with considerable feeling about his father's expectations for him. His father had never been satisfied with anything he had done. Mr. R. felt much the same about himself as he was growing up and as an adult.

> THERAPIST: So this man was saying, "You're not what you feel you should be."
>
> PATIENT: He was also saying—"And you haven't got what it takes to make it here." That's what hurt the most.

In subsequent interviews the patient returned to this theme repeatedly as though he were desensitizing himself to it. He also began to describe some improvement in his ability to work. Then he began to talk about his lack of communication with his wife. It became evident that this had been a major source of unhappiness for some time. He had buried himself in his work, spending long hours in the office. Even when he went home, he was likely to bring a briefcase full of paper work with him. When he became depressed and incapable of working as hard as he had before, the lack of a mutually supportive relation with her became painfully apparent. He described their courtship. He met her after being rejected by a young woman to whom he'd been engaged. She was available, interested in him, and seemed to have a very pleasant disposition.

> PATIENT: As I think about it, I never thought she was too bright, but she was very easy to get along with. And she wasn't stupid, you know. Just sort of quiet, didn't argue and was very warm. If I wanted to do something, it was O.K. with her, you know? But then I got busy and the kids came along, and she was busy with them, and we just never talked much. She was happy with it that way, I guess, and still is.
> THERAPIST: How do you know?
> PATIENT: Well, she doesn't really try to talk to me, you know.
> THERAPIST: But have you tried to talk to her?
> PATIENT: (*Silent for several seconds*) I guess I don't expect her to respond. (*Silent again*) You're saying I ought to try to talk with her.
> THERAPIST: No, I'm just saying that you haven't tried. I think you've cast her in a role that she may find comfortable and can live with, but may not be the only one she can take. But you seem to have felt this was how it should be—you busy with work and she busy with the kids and nothing between you.
> PATIENT: (*Incredulously*) You think I like it this way?
> THERAPIST: I didn't say that.
> PATIENT: But this is how I think it ought to be?
> THERAPIST: More like that. You expect it to be that way and act accordingly.

In the next session the patient spoke about the lack of communication between his parents when he was growing up. Soon after, he reported a long conversation with his wife about the distance that had developed between them that ended with a decision to try to do something about it. This was at about the fifteenth session.

Although treatment went on for about fifty sessions, or about a year, improvement was evident by the twentieth session. The later sessions were spent "working through" what he was beginning to learn about himself. He saw that his drive toward success through hard work, a demanding attitude toward himself and others, and an unawareness of his impact on others had denied him the satisfactions of good relations with his family and colleagues at work. Occasionally he would relate this to his father's attitude toward him. The therapist did not make that connection for him, however.

The therapist was usually supportive and asked questions chiefly for clarification or to get information for an interpretation or confrontation. Interpretations, used sparingly, tended to be about current matters rather than the past, though the patient sometimes responded with memories of similar events or relations from childhood and adolescence. Usually the patient talked about events of the week since the preceding appointment.

An example of an interpretation and the patient's response is given below. The patient had been talking about a younger man in his department. He described this man's "ineptitude" and a confrontation between them over a major error made by his subordinate.

> PATIENT: Well, I really let him have it. When I finished telling him what I thought of what he'd done, he looked very upset— kind of depressed. But after he left, I started to feel very bad. I thought, "Now he'll be demoralized and will do even worse, I shouldn't have done that."
>
> THERAPIST: Did you think he'd be upset by your comments before you made them?
>
> PATIENT: Well, not exactly. I did think I shouldn't be too rough.
>
> THERAPIST: But not about your effect on him—how he'd react?
>
> PATIENT: No, I never do.
>
> THERAPIST: Exactly. Because you're so tense about how your per-

formance will be judged by your boss, you lose sight of what the effect of your behavior will be on the man who reports to you.

PATIENT: (*After a pause*) I *was* very tense. I thought, "This goof will look terrible when the vice-president sees it, and he'll blame me." I was just thinking of myself.

Termination was broached in the following way.

PATIENT: I'm really getting along well now—feel much better. I think I understand how I was creating most of my own problems.

He went on to describe a recent commendation from the President of the company.

THERAPIST: It sounds like you may be almost ready to stop treatment. How do you feel about it?

PATIENT: I have to admit I've thought about it once or twice recently. You think we ought to quit?

THERAPIST: I suggest we set a termination date and see how that works. How about four weeks from now?

PATIENT: Sounds good to me.

Each of the last four sessions was devoted partly to the patient's feelings about termination. During the second last session, he expressed some doubts about it.

PATIENT: What if I get depressed again?

THERAPIST: You know my phone number. We can always have an appointment or two if you feel you need it. Or, we can even start up again with weekly sessions if we feel you need more treatment.

PATIENT: (*Obviously relieved*) Oh, I doubt that will be necessary.

Treatment ended uneventfully one week later.

Without special training in psychoanalytic therapy or one of its derivatives, the beginning therapist should generally limit his interpretations to relatively low levels of inference about current problems. Otherwise, there is the danger of substituting his own hypotheses for the patient's understanding. Too much emphasis on past events as causal factors of present-day behavior can encourage the patient to use the explanations as justification for continuing the problem behavior.

INQUIRY IN INSIGHT-AIMING PSYCHOTHERAPY

Insight therapies have been called *evocative therapy* by Frank (1961). In his view the essence of evocative methods lies in the therapist's fostering an atmosphere that encourages the patient to try to enlarge his self-knowledge, helping him to get to the root of problems and to attempt appropriate changes. The therapist's behavior in the therapy sessions encourages the patient to express himself with complete freedom. This requires an accepting, non-judgmental attitude on the part of the therapist. It also calls for a great deal of facilitation (as the term is defined in Chapter 2) from the therapist. But from time to time confrontations and questions are used as methods of inquiry to develop further the patient's insight.

Confrontation

In some situations confrontation may be the best method of inquiry. One such situation arises when a patient regularly fails to mention an important area of his life during therapy sessions. Another is anything in the patient's interaction with the therapist that reflects problems in the relation which are never mentioned.

> After several interviews, a new patient had described marital problems brought on partly by her job, some feelings of depression, concerns about the future but nothing about her work itself. She was 31 years old, married, and a legal secretary. After discussion of an argument with her husband when she had reached home late from work, the therapist commented on the lack of information volunteered about her work.
>
> THERAPIST: I notice that you never mention your job.
> PATIENT: (*After a relatively long silence*) I don't?
> THERAPIST: No. And your job had something to do with the argument you told me about.

PATIENT: (*Thoughtfully*) Yes, it did. (*Silent again*) Well, I told you that Harry is jealous of my boss. (*Silence*)

THERAPIST: Yes, you did.

PATIENT: (*Silent again*) He thinks I'm attracted to him and he gets upset about it. (*Silence*) The trouble is, I am attracted to him.

This led to a discussion of her defensiveness in the face of her husband's accusations.

When patients show toward the clinician feelings that may constitute a problem for them, a confrontation may often bring these feelings into focus and under discussion.

A 38-year-old woman who prepared public relations material for a university was very critical of the professors and administrators from whom she received the information for her publicity releases. Her criticisms were usually phrased in terms of the characteristics of people in a particular field or profession. Each time she criticized someone who was in a field in any way similar or related to that of the therapist, she would hasten to say that he (the therapist) was quite different.

THERAPIST: You know, I've noticed that whenever you say something critical about psychologists, physicians or anyone who does something close to what I do, you quickly assure me that it doesn't apply to me.

PATIENT: (*Tears coming to her eyes*) I guess I'm afraid you'll get angry and stop my treatment.

THERAPIST: Why would I do that?

PATIENT: Sometimes I get angry at you, too. But then I think, "I'd better not tell him or he'll get rid of me."

This led to a discussion of her great fear of expressing anger toward people whose relation with her was close and valued, an important theme in her life.

Another situation in which confrontation can be very useful is silence. When a patient is silent, there is no reason to interrupt the silence if the patient does not show signs of tension. Many patients are silent for several minutes at a time, and some may become silent for even longer periods. When a patient is silent but is expressing tension, depression, or other feelings non-verbally, confrontation can be an effective form of inquiry.

A patient has been describing his depression and feeling of failure. He had held an important supervisory position in his office until an associate, who had also been a close friend, was promoted to a post above him, and the importance of his job was reduced.

PATIENT: I taught him everything he knows, and now—(*Silence of about sixty seconds*)
THERAPIST: And now?
(*Silence—more than a minute. The patient looks more depressed and his chin quivers.*)
THERAPIST: You know, you look like you are about to cry.
(*Patient begins to weep silently. After another minute or two, he wipes his eyes.*)
PATIENT: I started to think about how he had used me. He got his promotion by exploiting me. Now he barely talks to me. I couldn't say it because I didn't want to cry in front of you.

Questions

When a discussion leaves some important questions unanswered in in the mind of the therapist, it is well to seek clarity. Ambiguity in describing feelings or incidents is one of the ways people avoid examining them. Most people seek to avoid pain—and the examination of problems can be painful, especially when it leads to awareness of embarrassing or unattractive aspects of one's behavior. Ambiguity in the patient's account can be dealt with by a confrontation about the sketchiness or lack of clarity, or by tactful questioning to clarify the picture. The example below is from a session with a 29-year-old airline stewardess who had not worked since incurring a minor head injury six months earlier. She had headaches, a stiff neck, and was depressed.

PATIENT: (*Describing events of the previous evening*) Then Tom came over and it was all very unsatisfactory. So I went to bed early.
THERAPIST: All very unsatisfactory?
PATIENT: Yes. He was awful. I did the best I could to make him

behave reasonably, and I just gave up. Anyway, I didn't sleep well, my head ached and my neck was stiff.

THERAPIST: I don't understand. What happened?

PATIENT: Oh, he wanted to go to a movie. (*Silence*)

THERAPIST: That's all that happened?

PATIENT: (*Reluctantly*) Well, no. I guess I was rather unpleasant about it.

THERAPIST: About going to a movie?

PATIENT: Well . . . actually I was being bitchy when he first came in. (*Silence*) Well, what really happened was that he suggested a movie when he saw what a bad mood I was in. But I couldn't get hold of myself and I kept on being cranky and finally he left. I guess I do that a lot.

THERAPIST: You didn't really want to tell me all of it, did you?

PATIENT: No. I can be very disagreeable sometimes. But I know it's a problem.

Sullivan's description of insight-aiming psychotherapy—as "facilitating the accession to awareness of information which will clarify for the patient the more troublesome aspects of his life" (1953)—is relevant here.

SUMMARY

Insight-oriented therapies, which originated in Freud's methods of psychoanalysis, seek to help the patient achieve greater awareness and understanding of his feelings and behavior. All of them aim to increase his ability to put his insights into words. Consequently, as Frank (1961) points out, they appeal to educated members of our society who place a high value on self-knowledge and verbal skills.

Whereas insight therapies are concerned with both the past and the present, the long-term therapies place somewhat more emphasis on the past, and utilize higher-inference interpretations than do the briefer insight therapies.

Also derived from psychoanalysis, particularly from its later development, are the process-oriented therapies to be discussed in Chapter 5.

REFERENCES

Alexander, F., and French, T. M. *Psychoanalytic Therapy: Principles and Application.* New York: Ronald Press, 1946.

Breuer, J., and Freud, S. *Studies on Hysteria* (1895). In *Standard Edition of the Complete Psychological Works of Sigmund Freud,* ed. by J. Strachey, Vol. II. London: Hogarth Press, 1958.

Frank, J. D. *Persuasion and Healing.* Baltimore: The Johns Hopkins Press, 1961.

Freud, S. "Remembering, Repeating and Working-Through" (Further Recommendations on the Technique of Psychoanalysis II). In *Standard Edition of the Complete Psychological Works of Sigmund Freud,* ed. by J. Strachey, Vol. XII. London: Hogarth Press, 1958.

Hollingshead, A., and Redlich, F. C. *Socio-economic Status and Mental Illness.* New York: Wiley, 1958.

Stein, M. I., ed. *Contemporary Psychotherapies.* New York: Free Press, 1961.

Stewart, Robert L. "Psychoanalysis and Psychoanalytic Psychotherapy." In *Comprehensive Textbook of Psychiatry II,* by A. Freedman, H. I. Kaplan, and B. J. Sadock. Baltimore: Williams and Wilkins, 1975.

Sullivan, H. S. *Conceptions of Modern Psychiatry,* p. 91. New York: W. W. Norton, 1953.

5

PROCESS-ORIENTED PSYCHOTHERAPY

Verbal communication can be analyzed at two levels: that of *content*—the actual information that is exchanged, and that of *process*—the manner in which the persons communicating with each other behave as they interact. In psychotherapy the clinician should be alert to both levels of communication. Often there is incongruity between the two, particularly on the part of the patient, who may be saying one thing but expressing something quite different in his manner. Signs of tension, anxiety, and depression may appear in the patient's behavior, even though never mentioned in his verbal account. The patient's speech—by its rhythm, intonations, and silences—his posture, and his facial expression all give indications of feelings and attitudes that may not be verbalized. The process, in fact, usually gives a more reliable picture than does the content of how the patient feels about the therapist. The manner in which the patient approaches the therapist and tries to structure the relation can be an important focus for the therapist's comments.

In process-oriented psychotherapy the therapist's attention is given primarily to the process rather than to the content of the patient's communications. The therapist is more likely to comment on the patient's behavior toward him than on what he is saying.

It is basically a here-and-now approach. The therapist is concerned primarily with what is going on during the therapy session itself.

As mentioned in Chapter 4, the content of patients' communications was the starting point for modern psychotherapy. Greatly influenced by his early experience with hysterical patients, Freud believed, at first that the therapist's task was to bring to consciousness repressed or unconscious material. But because of the unpredictability of the results of his early efforts to recover patients' memories, he became increasingly concerned with *feelings* and with the way patients behaved toward him. The concepts of defense, resistance, and transference, which were based on his observations of the therapist-patient relation, reflect this growing concern with the process of therapy in addition to the content of the patient's communications.

Wilhelm Reich considered his modification of psychoanalytic method, which he called "character analysis," a logical extension of Freud's proposal to deal with the "surface of the patient's mind." Reich was interested in the ways that a patient's attitudes and characteristic style of relating to others learned in his earliest social relations were reflected in his demeanor, bearing or carriage, gait, tone of voice, and other physical aspects of his behavior. Referring to these attributes as "character armor," he suggested that the therapist pay close attention to the physical expression of the patient's defenses (1948).

Otto Rank was probably the first process-oriented therapist. Along with many other therapists of his time, he started out as a student and disciple of Freud. He was also Freud's protégé and personal secretary for many years. In the middle 1920's, however, he began to differ with the Freudian theoretical position and to experiment with a variety of psychotherapy systems. Later he commented that whatever theory guided his interpretations of the patient's behavior at the time, the process was helpful to the patient. He concluded from this that the therapeutic element was something in the *relation*, rather than what he was saying. Rank finally arrived at the view that if the therapist attends only to the behavior occurring during therapy, and if the patient responds actively, then behavior patterns learned in earlier relations can be modified by the experience. In psychotherapy the patient's responses follow all his old patterns, but the key to change is that therapy provides a new situation where new learning can take place. The therapist helps the patient to recognize his responses as they are occurring and enlists the patient's "will" in efforts to modify his responses. Rank called his approach "will therapy" because he believed that the effect of a successful treatment was to strengthen the patient's "will to health" and independence (1936, 1964).

His position was further elaborated by Jessie Taft (1962) and Frederick Allen (1942)—the first a psychologist who became dean of a school of social work, the second a child psychiatrist—who first published their ideas in the 1930s. Taft and Allen stressed the importance of setting a termination date early in the treatment, so as to bring the problem of eventual separation from the therapist into the foreground of therapy. They shared with Rank the view that neurotic individuals are unable to define themselves as separate persons and wish to be very close to parent figures. Thus, facing and discussing feelings about separation in the therapeutic process itself could teach the patient how to cope with separation and the awareness of his separate identity.

Hellmuth Kaiser independently developed an approach somewhat similar to Rank's in intent, though different in style. Influenced by his training with Reich, he became convinced that the important element in psychotherapy was the interaction between patient and therapist; and he, too, felt that the therapist could work only with what goes on in the therapy session itself. Kaiser, however, focused on what he observed as a lack of congruity between content and process in the patient's communication with him. He felt that the neurotic individual has an unconscious desire to cling to an illusion that he is not a separate and distinct person responsible for himself. In order to maintain this he must create "an illusion of fusion" with others. To support such a relation, "duplicity of communication" is required of both partners. Each must hide any tendencies that do not fit the needs of the other, so that personal autonomy and true intimacy become impossible. In such relations the individual communicates more than one message at a time: a verbal message conveying how he wishes to appear to himself and to the other, and a non-verbal, which may express something quite different. During therapy the patient will behave in much the same way as in his relations with others.

This was described by Kaiser as follows:

> What the patient says is not quite representative of him, his own self, but something which the hearer experiences as distant, indirect, an artifact, not a straight-forward self-expression. (1955)

The therapist does not respond as the others do; instead, he brings to the patient's attention, through confrontation, the elements of his communicative behavior that strike a false note. In Kaiser's view, as in Rank's, this is a learning experience for the patient (1965). It is probable that the patient learns to communicate in a less "duplicitous" way than before, since a Kaiserian therapist would respond to direct communication in a manner that would be more satisfying to the patient than the confrontations. Moreover, Kaiser's therapy produces a situation that is rather ambiguous for the patient. He gave his patients few or no instructions, did not require that they tell him anything other than what they wished to tell, and made few requirements other than appearance at the therapy sessions. This tends to foster a wide range of adaptive social behavior, since such a therapist fails to meet the patient's expectations about the therapist's behavior.

To some extent all insight-oriented therapists behave this way, by failing to provide the degree of advice, direction, and control that many patients seek. For the patient this produces problems that are general to all social relations, including dealing with authority and with unsatisfying social responses. The patient tries his repertory of responses and develops new ones to solve these problems (Enelow and Adler, 1965). The response of the therapist provides social reinforcement of direct, or non-neurotic, communication. Social reinforcement of the new behavior by others then tends to perpetuate it.

A more recent variation of process-oriented psychotherapy that is somewhat closer to insight therapy is "transactional analysis." Developed by Eric Berne, this approach relies more heavily than Rank's or Kaiser's on interpretation and on a specific theory of behavior. Berne's theory of social behavior was based on his assumption that people seek recognition from others either through physical contact or a social response, which he termed "strokes." As he wrote, "A *stroke* may be used as the fundamental unit of social action" (1964). To elicit these "strokes" from others, people play "games."

Berne defines games as patterns of social behavior that are engaged in by two or more people and have sequences of verbal or physical actions and responses that can be described and classified and follow unspoken rules and constraints. Some of these rules are defined culturally; others are defined by tacit agreement of the persons involved. "Pastimes" are similar to games but less complex or more superficial. "Rituals" are still simpler, usually brief exchanges. Intimacy, on the other hand, is the most satisfying and "healthy" transaction (as contrasted with games). Games are characteristic of neurotics' relations or transactions, as well as of many superficial encounters. Berne wrote that "pastimes and games are substitutes for the real living of real intimacy" (1964). Berne's concept of games is thus similar to Kaiser's concept of the social behavior of neurotic persons.

Berne also utilized a concept of "ego states," which he defined as "sets of coherent behavior patterns with related sets of feelings." Everyone has three of these. One corresponds to the person's parents' behavior toward him; another, to his most integrated or mature behavior and ability to appraise reality; and the third, to his earlier childhood behavior and attitudes. He called these "parent," "adult," and "child" ego states. In any given social interaction, a person can exhibit any of them, or shift from one to another.

In transactional analysis the therapist deals with behavior in the session—often a group therapy session. Confrontations and interpretations are made as to the games being played and to the "ego state" the patient is exhibiting. The therapist's work is to point out what is going on in the patient's games and to label them for what they are: ritualistic transactions, often repetitious, superficially plausible, with concealed motivation and an ulterior aim. The transactional analyst also uses the concept of "life script," a term describing the inflexible responses of neurotic persons who tend to play a limited number of games repeatedly.

Another important process-oriented approach to psychotherapy, that of Carl R. Rogers (1956), was also influenced by Otto Rank. Rogers, however, rejected the medical model for understanding disorders of behavior, and saw psychiatric illness as "learned behaviors." In keeping with this view, he called the person seeking his help a client, and labeled his type of therapy "client-centered counseling" to get away from the notion of treatment of an illness.

In Rogers's theory "the self" is the organizing principle of a person's social behavior, and this self tends to maintain a position of consistency. This is a way of saying that people have a consistent view of themselves and tend to reject thoughts, feelings, values, acts, and potential experiences not consistent with this view. Accordingly, they cannot allow themselves to recognize some of their feelings. More, they cannot permit themselves to have experiences that might threaten this self-concept. The client-centered therapist assumes that his client can learn new behavior if he is given the opportunity to find insight into his own feelings and thoughts, and that he will achieve insights that will result in positive changes in his life if he can explore his problems with a therapist who has the following characteristics:

1. The therapist can be himself (is genuine).
2. The therapist feels a warm, positive, accepting attitude toward the client.
3. The therapist has a reasonably accurate, empathic understand-

ing of the client's inner world without losing the separateness of his own identity, i.e., awareness of the difference between the client's and his inner world.

The client should then perceive the genuine acceptance and empathy of the therapist. In relation with such a therapist, the client can allow himself to feel certain things and to examine alternatives of behavior that heretofore he has been unable to.

The Rogerian therapist aims to be perceived by his client as dependable. He also aims to communicate unambiguously. He believes that he cannot help the client if he does not feel positively toward such client. An essential point in Rogers's views, as in Rank's and in Kaiser's, is that the therapist must behave in a way that respects the client's personal autonomy—i.e., he does not impose his ideas or values on the client. While the therapist must enter the client's world by understanding what he is experiencing, he must do so in a sensitive, non-judgmental way, so that he is not perceived as a threat. The therapist then tells his client his perception of what the client is trying to say or seems to be experiencing. This involves a great deal of support, confrontation, and interpretation of what the client seems to be feeling during the session. According to Rogers, if this is effective, the client's rigid psychological functioning aimed at avoiding experiences that threaten his self-concept will gradually become more flexible and open the way to new experiences. This calls for considerable restating of what the client has said or appears to be communicating, verbally and non-verbally.

The following case demonstrates a Kaiserian approach to process-oriented psychotherapy.

> Mrs. Sharon T., a 32-year-old married woman, was referred to a psychotherapist by her family doctor because of an intractable peptic ulcer. In the initial interview the patient talked at some length about her present situation and her history. She was one of two children. She had been raised by a nursemaid and hardly knew her own parents. When she was with them, however, there was much demonstration of affection in a rather artificial way.

She married at 19 and had two children. Her husband was a professional man who had recently had a heart attack. Though somewhat undemonstrative, he had ordinarily been attentive, but after his heart attack he became extremely inattentive, self-centered, and irascible. She found him annoyingly demanding and uninterested in her. Under conditions of stress in the past she had had two transitory peptic ulcers that responded well to medical management. This time, however, her ulcer continued to be active and symptomatic despite months of treatment. She became depressed and indecisive, and was preoccupied with her husband's coldness and irritability.

In the initial interview the therapist was impressed that the patient recited her history of the many wrongs done to her by her husband with an absolutely expressionless face. Even more noticeable was the fact that when she smiled or when she wept her eyes did the weeping, or her mouth did the smiling, but her general facial musculature took no part. This led to a very wooden and unconvincing expression. Her account indicated that she felt no internal difficulty (other than stomach ache). Her problems, as she saw them, were thrust upon her by a disturbed and disturbing husband.

Her second interview began:

PATIENT: What is it that I am expected to do here?

THERAPIST: (*After a moment*) Nothing, really, if I understand your question. It sounds like you are saying: "What do you want me to do?" There's nothing that I want you to do.

She looked puzzled. After a moment, she shrugged as though to say, nonverbally, "What a strange man this is," and began to talk about what had happened since her previous appointment. This consisted of a detailed account of her husband's self-centered behavior.

After about twenty minutes the therapist became so aware of the curious woodenness of expression that had been apparent in the first interview that he could hardly concentrate on the patient's words.

THERAPIST: You know, it is a very interesting thing that when you smile, nothing takes part in the smile expect your mouth.

The patient looked uncomprehending but, after a moment, shrugged and went on talking. Soon tears came to her eyes, while her facial expression remained unchanged.

THERAPIST: I noticed that you were crying just then, but nothing moved in your face while you cried.

PATIENT: (*Irritated*) What do you mean by that?

THERAPIST: Just what I said. It is a kind of odd sensation to speak with someone whose face shows as little feeling as yours does, even when you seem to feel something strongly.

PATIENT: But I don't understand. What am I expected to do with that?

THERAPIST: Nothing, really, I guess. I just wanted you to know how curious this looked to me.

This might be said to characterize the interaction between patient and therapist throughout the course of therapy. The atmosphere of the sessions was friendly. The patient talked about various things that were going on in her life. The therapist, in turn, commented in non-judgmental terms on behavior during the appointments that struck him as incongruous or artificial. Even though she never seemed to understand just what point the therapist intended to make, she always gave close attention to his comments. There was a progressive change in her behavior, not only during the interviews but also at home and in other places as she described it.

There was a remarkable similarity of theme whenever she spoke. Usually she complained about the hardship she suffered because of the unreasonable behavior of someone else. At first these complaints focused on the self-centered churlishness of her husband. Sometimes the subject was her mother's unwillingness to inconvenience herself for the patient. As time went on, her husband was less often the subject of the complaint. More often it was the husband's business partner, her in-laws, her son, or the wives of her husband's colleagues. From time to time the therapist commented on this, taking one of the following points of view: (a) "You speak as though everything that happened to you was at the instigation [or due to the pressure] of someone else," or (b) "Curious—today it is your mother-in-law. Last week it was your husband's partner. But the subject really remains the same."

At times the tone of her voice and her general manner were

those of one performing a task out of a sense of duty but without real interest in it. That is, she spoke as though she were *required* to come to the office, *required* to speak, had to prod herself to go through the motions. The therapist described this to her. At first it annoyed her; later she was amused. (At herself? at him?—The therapist was never certain.)

Gradually the stiffness in her manner relaxed. Her general appearance became more animated. She spoke of herself and how *she* felt more often, about the unfairness of others less.

After about fifteen months of treatment, Mrs. T. came in one day and said something like this: "I feel very much better. I have not had stomach pains in more than five or six months." (This was the first indication the therapist had that she was no longer experiencing ulcer symptoms.) As she went on,

> I cannot explain what it was that did it. I talked it over with my husband, and he agrees with me. Neither of us can understand why these silly inconsequential things that you say could possibly have helped me. But whatever it was that you did, it did help. I feel like a different person, and everybody says I've changed in many ways. My husband says I am more human than I used to be. So, thank you very much. I won't be coming any more after this week.

An accidental opportunity for a follow-up occurred some two years later when the therapist met the patient and her husband at a party. She greeted the therapist with: "I can never thank you enough for what you did for me, even though I don't understand how you did it. I have been feeling fine ever since."

A second example of process-oriented therapy is the case of Mr. C.L., a 37-year-old married social worker who complained of a feeling of discontent and an inability to enjoy anything.

> Mr. C.L. worked in a social agency where most of the other social workers were friendly with each other and "spoke the same language." He felt himself to be the outsider, not accepted by the others. His fear of disapproval led him to phrase things very cautiously. He "over-prepared" casework reports to avert any possible criticism, and felt that he must do better work than anyone else.

Yet he procrastinated in completing all reports. He was constantly alert to any suggestion that he was being treated unfairly or being patronized.

In treatment he found it almost impossible to state things without being circuitous or evasive. At first he watched for signs that the therapist looked down on him and for insincerity or authoritarian qualities in the therapist. His manner of phrasing things made it appear as though he was attempting to state everything he felt in a way that made his position impossible to criticize. He became particularly uneasy in trying to express negative feelings or criticism of the therapist.

The therapist first described to the patient some of his tortuous ways of expressing himself and told him of the difficulty he had in following his obsessive detail. For example, after a particularly detailed and hard-to-follow account, this interchange occurred:

THERAPIST: You know, I listened very carefully to you, just now. For a while I understood what you were describing. But as you added detail after detail, I began to lose track and before long I was more involved with the way you were telling the incident than with what happened.

PATIENT: You lost me?

THERAPIST: No, it felt more like you lost me—that is, you seemed more concerned with how much you were telling me than with making yourself understandable.

PATIENT: (*Pause*) Oh . . . I see. Well, let me try again.

This time his account was a little less detailed and more clear.

Another example of a process-oriented interchange is the following tape-recorded excerpt from a therapy session.

The patient is a 35-year-old unmarried accountant who suffered from shyness, extreme loneliness, and feelings of depression. Because his unhappiness was at times so extreme that he might stay away from work and remain in bed all day, he lost several jobs in succession. Finally realizing that he needed help, he applied to a psychiatric clinic for therapy. In the treatment sessions he was guarded and often uncommunicative. At times he remained silent for five or even ten minutes. One day the following dialogue took place:

PATIENT: I had an interesting experience Friday. I took—went to court with a traffic ticket that I got . . . uh . . . a month or

60 ELEMENTS OF PSYCHOTHERAPY

so ago in which . . . in which I felt that I didn't deserve it, and evidently the Judge felt so too because he came to a not-guilty verdict. But the thing that shook me up a little in this affair was that the police officer who had given me the ticket did a little lying in court here and it didn't affect matters, I don't think; in fact, if anything, it made him . . . it hurt him, I believe, but . . . well, one reason I brought this up was this last week we talked a little about how I'm suspicious of people in a way.

THERAPIST: Hm . . .

PATIENT: Well, this is a sort of thing that . . . (*pause*) . . . leads me to that conclusion that I don't quite . . . quite trust people. His lie was only to the effect that I was very derogatory toward him—told him he didn't know what he was doing and . . . and so forth, at the time he gave me the ticket, and . . . uh . . . which was not true at all. Uh, then I gave him an out on it . . . asked if he didn't confuse this ticket with some other ticket and he said "No, positively not" and then I asked him . . . I had questioned his saying that my driver's license had expired at the time he gave me the ticket and . . . he had said, "Well, no, this is the way it is and it has expired, and, uh, if you don't . . . you'll have to see the Judge if you don't believe it." And so I asked him if this was what had made him think I made derogatory remarks and "No, that wasn't it," he said, so I don't know . . . but anyway it made me damn mad! Er, you . . . it's a very minor thing and yet it's, uh . . .

THERAPIST: It seems to mean a great deal to you.

PATIENT: Well, I think it does because I value honesty very highly . . . uh . . . much more so I guess than most people . . . (*pause*) . . . The thing here that I don't know about is that if the . . . if the fellow was maliciously lying, if he consciously knew he was lying in this case, then . . . then that really, uh, irritates me. It's possible that he just didn't recall the circumstances and he thought that this was what happened; this is perhaps not so bad but this I can never know. (*Lengthy pause*) Well, anyway so it seems that . . . (*pause*) . . . that, uh, (*pause*) an awful lot of people will do things like this and tell little lies when it's to their advantage and it can't be proven otherwise. (*Lengthy pause*)

THERAPIST: And you find this kind of depressing?

PATIENT: Yeah.

THERAPIST: Cause you look awfully unhappy when you say that.

PATIENT: I do! It's, uh . . . (*pause very long*). I know . . . uh, I'd like to think that, uh, it is possible to believe just about anything that anybody says to you but it isn't . . . (*pause*) not just . . . unintentional, uh, unintentionally being misleading, that is . . . this is quite a different thing from doing it purposely. Hm . . . (*pause, very long*). Well (*cough*) anyway I think this point about my being a little suspicious of people and not being willing to trust them is pretty important here.

THERAPIST: Yeah, and I have the feeling also that you in essence say—to me today—"But of course this is the only intelligent, rational attitude one can have: see how the traffic cop acted when I was in court?"

PATIENT: You mean I think that *to be* a little suspicious is appropriate, eh?

THERAPIST: Yeah.

PATIENT: I know I feel that way. I guess I . . . uh . . . am suspicious and so forth, and . . . this is probably where I go overboard a little that I'm probably a little too suspicious, uh, and when something like this happens, then I . . . I know that there is, uh, bad business going on and it certainly appears to be maliciously intended and not just . . . uh . . . a misunderstanding or something . . . uh, it does upset me . . . a hell of a lot! (*Pause*) Right!

THERAPIST: You were disappointed that he was not honest?

PATIENT: Yeah . . . yeah, certainly. I guess so . . . So I know I don't . . . (*Pause*) . . . I think the thing here is that I don't . . . (*pause*) . . . want to become less honest . . . (*pause*) but what I do need to do maybe is to . . . (*long pause*) . . . to not, uh, have disrespect for people to the extent that I do when I find that they're not as honest as I feel they should be maybe. (*Very long pause*) It sounds like I'm bragging or something about being real honest . . . (*very long pause*) . . .

THERAPIST: You know, I had the distinct impression there, uh, that you got kind of embarrassed by what then appeared to be a kind of bragging on your part about how honest you were.

PATIENT: (*Very long pause*) I suppose so . . . you're probably right . . . I don't know . . . (*very long pause*) . . . but I . . . I think . . . it isn't . . . that I feel I am bragging here

exactly . . . uh . . . (*very long pause*) . . . I think the thing
that embarrasses me is that I . . . suddenly realize . . . uh,
that I may be all wrong in this. (*Lengthy pause*)

THERAPIST: I'm not sure what you mean when you say you may
be all wrong in this . . .

PATIENT: Well, it . . . I'm sort of (*mumble*) . . . the feeling I
. . . I sort of felt that I was projecting myself as being, uh,
Diogenes looking for the honest man or something, and it isn't
. . . again I'm not, uh, exceptional . . . exceptionally honest,
just I would say . . . somewhat more than the majority of the
people.

THERAPIST: That still embarrasses you, doesn't it?—even to say that
much, I would think. You know I . . . the impression that I
gather is that you don't really feel free to say what you think
and you are somewhat deterred by what I might think of what
you might say.

PATIENT: Yeah . . . that's certainly true . . . of course, this
holds for all people that I might be talking to and, or, most
people much more than it does with you fellows.

THERAPIST: That's right . . .

PATIENT: (*After long pause*) I don't know . . . I'm sort of
afraid to, uh, promote my own good qualities for some reason . . .

SUMMARY

To maintain a pure process-oriented stance in psychotherapy is difficult for most beginning therapists. Many patients require considerable support, or at times direct intervention by means of suggestion and interpretation. Yet certain principles of process-oriented
psychotherapy can be applied in most types of psychotherapy.
Thus,

1. In general, it is more useful to discuss what is going on within
   the hour, and what is happening in the immediate present, than
   to direct the patient's attention toward the past.
2. When a patient's behavior and affect are incongruous, or when
   there is a contradiction between his words and his non-verbal
   expression of feelings, a gentle confrontation is always helpful.

Similarly, when the patient cannot communicate, but is non-verbally expressing strong feelings, such a confrontation can be very useful.

3. A therapist's comments on lack of clarity or directness in the patient's communication can advance the patient's understanding by prompting him to explain his feelings, clarifying them for himself.

4. The therapist should conduct himself so as to promote a mature relation between himself and the patient. He should be alert to attempts by the patient to develop a relation in which the patient takes a kind of dependent, child-like role.

5. The therapist should behave in a way that encourages the patient to take responsibility for himself, his words, and his actions.

Almost all insight-oriented therapy is process-oriented to some degree, but much less emphasis is placed on insight in most process-oriented therapy, least of all on insight into the past.

REFERENCES

Allen, F. H. *Psychotherapy with Children*. New York: W. W. Norton, 1942.

Berne, E. *Games People Play*. New York: Grove Press, 1964.

————. *Principles of Group Treatment*. New York: Oxford University Press, 1966.

Enelow, A. J., and Adler, L. M. Foreword to *Effective Psychotherapy; The Contribution of Hellmuth Kaiser*, ed. by L. B. Fierman. New York: Free Press, 1965.

Freud, S. "Remembering, Repeating and Working-Through" (Further Recommendations on the Technique of Psychoanalysis II). In *Standard Edition of the Complete Psychological Works of Sigmund Freud*, ed. by J. Strachey, Vol. XII. London: Hogarth Press, 1958.

Kaiser, H. *Effective Psychotherapy: The Contribution of Hellmuth Kaiser*, ed. by L. B. Fierman. New York: Free Press, 1965.

————. "The Problem of Responsibility in Psychotherapy." *Psychiatry* 18:205–11, 1955.

Rank, O. *Will Therapy* and *Truth and Reality*. New York: Knopf, 1964 (originally published separately in 1936).

Reich, W. "On Character Analysis." In *The Psychoanalytic Reader*, ed. by R. Fliess. New York: International Universities Press, 1948.

Rogers, C. R. "Client-Centered Therapy. A Current View." In *Progress in Psychotherapy I*, ed. by F. Fromm-Reichmann and J. L. Moreno. New York: Grune and Stratton, 1956.

Taft, J. *The Dynamics of Therapy in a Controlled Relationship*. New York: Dover Publications, 1962.

6

SUPPORTIVE PSYCHOTHERAPY

Supportive therapy is probably the most widely used type of psychotherapy in medical settings. Moreover, all successful psychotherapy seems to have a supportive element. It is doubtful that a patient will continue in therapy if he or she does not experience a feeling of support. In simple terms, a patient who does not sense some warmth or concern in the therapist is less likely to receive help than one who does.

This issue was explored in an essay by Carl Rogers (1961). After reviewing some comparative studies of psychotherapy, he concluded that patients who perceived their therapists as impersonal, whether by reason of the therapeutic method or as a natural function of the therapist's personality, were less likely to have had a successful outcome than those who felt trust in the therapist and understood by him. Rogers concluded that it is the attitudes and feelings of the therapist rather than his theoretical orientation that is important. Mutual liking and respect between therapist and patient appeared to be closely associated with a successful outcome. Rogers recommended the term "helping relationship" instead of "psychotherapy," defining this as a relation in which "at least one of the parties has the intent of promoting the growth, development, maturity, improved functioning, and improved coping with life of the other."

Support was defined in Chapter 2 as any action of the therapist that communicates his interest in, liking for, or understanding of the patient and that helps give the patient a feeling of security in the relation. In supportive psychotherapy this is the principal activity of the therapist. As support is often effective in reducing anxiety and alleviating depression, it can relieve psychological distress that interferes with problem solving. Once the stress of crisis situations is reduced by supportive therapy, a patient may be able to cope with the problems that led to his emotional crises.

Although supportive statements and actions are naturally the most important aspect of the therapist's behavior in supportive psychotherapy, they will not achieve their aim if the therapist's *attitude* is not also supportive. A supportive attitude is compounded of a number of elements, notably: 1. genuine interest in and concern for the patient; 2. a feeling of warmth and friendliness toward the patient; 3. a desire to be helpful; and 4. maintenance of sufficient reserve, so that the therapist remains clearly aware that he is engaging in a helping relation (Enelow and Wexler, 1966). This enumeration is similar to Rogers's description of the therapist's role in a helping relationship: the therapist must be perceived by the other person as trustworthy, dependable, and consistent; he must be expressive and communicate unambiguously; he must hold attitudes of warmth, caring, liking, interest, and respect toward the other person; and he must be able to see the other's feelings in much the way the client does.

It is of course improbable that any therapist can like all his patients. This need not prevent treatment, though it is probably not possible to be genuinely supportive toward a person he actively dislikes. Concern, interest, warmth, and dependability do not presuppose actual affection for the patient. What counts is the patient's perception of the therapist. Since the need for demonstrable warmth from others varies from patient to patient, the ability to provide support to a given patient seems more a function of the therapist's personality than of the specific techniques he uses. When a therapist is perceived by his patients as strong, trustworthy, and competent, this reflects personal characteristics such as poise, self-confidence, and skill in communication. These personal attributes, when a therapist has them, are in themselves quite effective in reducing a patient's distress.

The most common reason for seeking psychotherapy is a problem with personal relations, a problem caused either by loss of a significant relationship or failure to achieve satisfaction through closeness. As Kaiser (1965) has written:

> Patients are lonely persons. Many of them are literally isolated and have few contacts with people, but even those who move in a circle of friends, have wives and children, parents and other relatives around them, are at least alone with their neurotic problems because these problems cannot be shared with other people.

He went on to say that they come to a therapist's office because they want to break out of this isolation. The depression, anxiety, or alienation reported by most patients in part reflects this isolation. A supportive relationship with a therapist may alleviate such symptoms merely by reducing the isolation and attendant sense of loneliness.

In supportive therapy the psychotherapist should encourage the patient to talk about current problems and difficulties. After the initial data-gathering interviews, attention should not be focused on past events except when the patient spontaneously describes some similarity between current and past problems. If the patient has difficulty in talking, the therapist should be facilitative (see Chapter 2). Long silences should be avoided. Confrontations should be used sparingly, and usually to facilitate the patient's verbal communication, as when he is silent but non-verbally indicates feelings such as sadness or tension.

Among the means of giving a patient support are the following: sympathetic listening and communication, encouragement, reassurance, guidance, and at times family counseling sessions to supplement individual therapy. Also, directions may be used to encourage changes in behavior.

In the following example, the therapist maintains a continuously supportive attitude and makes use of supportive remarks, encouragement to try new courses of action, and words of praise for actions that tend to increase the patient's self-esteem.

Mrs. R.M. was a 45-year-old married woman with two grown children who had both left home several years before. About seven or eight months before consulting the therapist, she had become aware that her husband was infatuated with another woman. He confessed this to her in order to relieve his own guilt feelings. The husband insisted that he had had no sexual relations with the other woman, although he had met her "for a drink" on several occasions. He had, however, begun to feel increasingly guilty and felt he had to tell his wife about it.

Mrs. M. became quite upset and demanded that he terminate the relation. He did so, expressing a great deal of remorse for his behavior, as well as relief that the "affair" was over. Nonetheless, Mrs. M., who was angry at first, became increasingly depressed. She was unable to get the image out of her mind of her husband and the "other woman" sitting together or having a drink. Also, she suspected that sexual activity had taken place between them. She became obsessed with the idea of seeing the "other woman." On at least one occasion she went to the bar where they had met, hoping to catch sight of her. Depressed, she consulted her family doctor and asked him for tranquilizers or sedatives. He refused to prescribe them, out of fear that she might be suicidal, and instead referred her to a psychotherapist.

When first seen, Mrs. M. was moderately depressed, quite angry with her husband and upset about his lack of loyalty. She felt she could no longer trust him. She talked of her depression, resentment, and jealousy of the "other woman." The following exchange occurred:

PATIENT: I am so upset at him that I really believe the only answer for me is to divorce him. What do you think?
THERAPIST: You must be very angry with him.
PATIENT: Yes, I am. I don't know whether I am angrier at him, though, or at her. Maybe I should leave him and let him go to her, if that's what he wants.

THERAPIST: Is that what he says he wants?

PATIENT: No. In fact, I've offered to leave him and let him go to her. But he says she's not the woman he wants to live with. He says it was an infatuation. He feels that we got married at a very young age and that he had some kind of adolescent need to play around. He wants to live with me for the rest of his life, not her. That doesn't make me feel any better. If he felt that way, why did he have anything to do with her?

THERAPIST: I can see that thinking about that makes you very angry. But I don't think you should make such decisions about your marriage right now. It would be better to sort things out first.

PATIENT: Well, I suppose you're right. Anyway I don't feel like undertaking anything major at this time. (*She smiled for the first time during this appointment.*)

In this session, the therapist is supportive ("You must be very angry with him") as well as directive, advising Mrs. M. to wait and "sort things out," and the patient feels relief that she does not have to make a difficult decision.

During the early sessions, Mrs. M. spent most of her time expressing her anger, saying things like, "How could he *do* that to me." In her view she had been very good to her husband over the years, subordinating all her needs to his. She frequently described uncomfortable evenings she spent with him at the home of another couple. She found the man disagreeable and the woman boring, and yet her husband and the other man enjoyed each other's company. They spent their time discussing Country and Western music, which did not interest Mrs. M. in the least. The two men often went into another room to listen to records, leaving her with the woman, with whom she could find nothing to talk about.

PATIENT: And that's the kind of thing I would do. I went to concerts to hear music that I didn't like. But whenever I suggested that we go to the theater or to a musical comedy, he would say he wasn't interested, and I never pushed it. And after all that, he could turn around and do *this* to me!

THERAPIST: I can see how much that thought upsets you.

PATIENT: Well, I think it is about time that I began to assert myself. I think it would make me feel better.

THERAPIST: I wouldn't be surprised if it did. Why not try it?

PATIENT: I would like to see "My Fair Lady" before its run ends. I'm going to just go out and buy two tickets and tell him we're going to see it. What do you think of that?

THERAPIST: Sounds like that might make you feel better about yourself.

PATIENT: Maybe he'd respect me more if I stood up for what I wanted once in a while.

THERAPIST: (*Warmly*) Maybe he would.

Here the therapist uses support to encourage the patient to undertake a new type of behavior that promises to enhance her self-esteem and reduce her depression. In this case, that was the effect.

At the next session the patient reported with great satisfaction that she had purchased the tickets, confronted her husband with her intention that they attend the performance and found, to her surprise, that he put up no objection.

THERAPIST: Good for you!

PATIENT: I feel better than I have in a long time. Maybe he felt he could go out with that woman because he had no respect for me. It doesn't pay to be a doormat, I've decided.

As therapy continued, the patient described her changing relationship with her husband. At first tentatively, then with increasing confidence, she became more assertive. She reported feeling more honest and, as a result, prouder of herself. Then she began to reflect on some of the things that might have caused her husband to become interested in other women. She had always been more sensitive to her husband's needs than he to hers. When one of their children had died in adolescence about ten years earlier, Mrs. M. became somewhat depressed and withdrew from her husband. There was little communication and no sexual relation for nearly a year. After that she slowly returned to her former responsiveness, except that, while she had always been rather compliant, she now did not ever voice her own wishes but allowed her husband to make all decisions. She thought that this might have been in response to her feelings of guilt for having turned away from him in her grief. Looking back, she saw that her behavior must have made her colorless and unexciting, and encouraged her husband to pay still less attention to her emotional needs.

After about five months of therapy, Mrs. M. reported that she was feeling very much better. On one occasion she brought her husband to a session. Mr. M. reported that there had been a change in their relation. His wife demanded more attention and concern from him and was more assertive, but he preferred the new situation to the old. After six months of therapy, the patient reported that she and her husband were spending more time together and sharing each other's interests to a greater degree. Therapist and patient agreed to terminate the treatment, and then had two concluding sessions consisting of progress reports from the patient about the improvement in her feelings and in her marital relations. The therapist ended the session by saying, "It seems to me that you're getting along fine. I have confidence that you will be able to handle things as they arise. But if you should have trouble, don't hesitate to call and make an appointment."

When patients are anxious and depressed, the problems they face may seem insurmountable. Decisions are difficult to make, and taking action appears to be nearly impossible. Failure to cope with the problems increases the patient's sense of despair, leading to intensification of the symptoms. Sometimes this vicious circle can be broken by directive measures. Suggesting and strongly supporting behavior that helps the patient take coping measures that he or she has put to use successfully in the past may reduce the patient's discomfort. To be able to take constructive action is in itself reassuring. This strategy is often adopted in crisis intervention.

A useful adjunct to directive measures is the diary, especially when a patient finds it hard to talk or has difficulty describing his daily activities. The patient is instructed to describe the principal activities of his day. If a particular symptom is one of the reasons the patient sought therapy, each occurrence should be noted, including the circumstances. Troublesome events or feelings should be noted. This record can give clues to the probable precipitants of symptoms, can make the patient more aware of his behavior with others and responses to them, and can help suggest new courses of action, as in the following case example:

Mrs. A.B. was a 48-year-old married woman with no children. She and her husband were both employed. About a year before therapy started, Mrs. B. began to have menopausal symptoms, gradually became depressed, and had to stop working. As a result she was at home a great deal. She spent much of her time pacing about, staring out the window, feeling demoralized and worthless. Productive work had always been of great importance to her. Now she began to feel that she would never be able to work again. Her husband was understanding and supportive at first. In time, however, her constant need for reassurance and support wore him down and he began to spend more time away from her—and this deepened her depression and loneliness. Though she had never been alcoholic, she began to drink to the point of moderate intoxication each day. Finally, her husband took her to their family physician, who referred her to a psychotherapist after ascertaining that medical treatment for the menopausal symptoms was not indicated.

At her first appointment Mrs. B. described the gradual onset of depression over the past year, and how it interfered with her work. She found it difficult to concentrate, felt lethargic and unmotivated, and began to dread going to work—and then became even more depressed. Her concerns centered upon menopause and the fear that soon she would no longer be sexually attractive to her husband. Without children she was afraid there would soon be nothing to hold them together. Mrs. B. had little to say except when encouraged to keep speaking or when asked a question. At other times she fell silent, staring at the floor. Occasionally she looked at the therapist in a manner that suggested a plea for help. After one period of silence, the therapist made the following observation and suggestion:

THERAPIST: I can see that you are very depressed. I also feel that your inactivity is making you feel worse.

PATIENT: I know, Doctor. I feel terrible when I am doing nothing. I've always been a hard worker and I can't stand being idle and unproductive.

THERAPIST: I think it is important that you begin to get as busy as you can, and as soon as possible. To begin with, I want you to keep a diary of what you do.

The therapist went on to describe how the diary should be kept. Principal activities of each day were to be recorded, and their duration. If her depression varied in depth, degrees of intensity were to be noted, and the circumstances. Reactions to other people were to be recorded, and also her alcohol intake.

At the next appointment the patient brought her diary, which indicated that she was doing little or nothing and that she was drinking about two ounces of vodka every few hours. Routine household chores were being done by her husband. The therapist then reiterated his view that she would begin to feel better if she tried to become more active. With the patient's concurrence the therapist assigned some simple tasks, which included preparing a meal and doing some household chores. A list of the proposed activities was made. Then the following exchange took place:

THERAPIST: Now, every day I want you to choose one of these tasks and work at it. Don't be discouraged if you don't do it well. You have to begin with whatever you can do and gradually improve your ability to work. Then your interest in things will begin to return as you become more active. And I want you to record the activities in your diary in addition to what you are now recording.

PATIENT: Oh, I don't think I can do it.

THERAPIST: I know how you must feel, that this is all too much for you, but I think you can do it. I have confidence in you. It doesn't matter if you don't do very much at first. However little you do, it will be helpful to you.

The following week the patient's diary reflected a small increase in her activity. The therapist responded with warm praise, reassurance as to her ability to handle more activity, and continuing support. The weekly sessions that followed were confined mostly to accounts of her activities, praise for accomplishments, and statements by the therapist of his conviction that she would improve, if she kept working on it. After about four weeks, the matter of her alcohol consumption was taken up. From both her diary and her husband's account, the therapist was aware that her alcohol intake, formerly quite small, had increased markedly during the last six months.

THERAPIST: I see that you are drinking about 12 ounces of vodka a day.

PATIENT: It helps me sleep. It seems to calm me down, and I don't feel quite so depressed after I take a drink.

THERAPIST: I can understand that. Alcohol is a sedative. But it also slows you down. And when it wears off you must feel worse.

PATIENT: When I feel the tension coming back, I take another drink.

THERAPIST: Exactly. But at that point your tension is worse than if you hadn't had a drink. So you're not just drinking to fight your tension and depression. You're also drinking to fight the effects of the previous drinks. I want you to stop drinking right now before you lose control of it.

PATIENT: I guess I can do it. I didn't drink every day until a few months ago.

THERAPIST: Good. I know it will help.

Mrs. B. reluctantly agreed. Despite an increase in feelings of tension for the first few days, she was able to stop drinking altogether—probably because the heavy alcohol intake had begun only recently. After the increased tension diminished, she noted a lessening of her depression and an increase in the level of her daily activity.

The diary's primary functions were to make the patient aware of what she was doing each day and to provide a focus for discussion, helping her overcome her difficulty in talking. As an activity in itself, keeping the diary helped ease the patient's sense of being idle and unproductive. Finally, its record of increasing activity gave her tangible evidence of improvement. This in turn enhanced her self-esteem.

As Mrs. B. improved, she began to talk more about her feelings about her age, her fear of losing her husband, and her sense of purposelessness in life. The therapist listened, offered support and occasionally some reassurance about her fears.

PATIENT: I know it's silly. My husband gives me no reason to think I'll lose him. Now that I can talk to him more, he's more like he used to be with me. But I keep thinking he'll get tired of all this one of these days and find someone younger and more energetic.

THERAPIST: As I see it, he hasn't given you any reason to feel that.

PATIENT: No, he hasn't.

THERAPIST: Isn't he getting older just as fast as you are?

PATIENT: Yes, but he doesn't act it, the way I do.

THERAPIST: Well, you have evidence that you're getting more active and energetic again, and I believe you will continue to improve. Getting older and recognizing that your body is changing is something we all must cope with. Your husband is dealing with the same problem. It's somthing you can talk about to each other.

At her next appointment, Mrs. B. reported that she had discussed her fears and her feelings about aging with her husband and felt relieved when he responded positively to her.

Mrs. B.'s depression slowly lifted as she became more active. She began to take on more complex tasks and started thinking about returning to work. The therapist encouraged this. One day, feeling more confidence in herself, she phoned her employer, who was delighted to hear from her and encouraged her to come back to work. At the next session, the therapist supported this.

PATIENT: He was very understanding. He said he was glad I was feeling better and hoped I'd be coming back soon. They miss me!

THERAPIST: That must have felt very good.

PATIENT: Oh, it did. I'd like to try it.

THERAPIST: Sounds like a good idea.

After returning to work, Mrs. B. continued in therapy for several more months. She began to talk about her responses to other people at work. Her social life expanded as she resumed entertaining friends at home and accepting their invitations. With the therapist's support and encouragement, she continued to increase her activity and to improve. The frequency of her sessions was reduced to twice and then once a month. Approximately one year after the beginning of therapy, regular appointments were discontinued.

Supportive psychotherapy is less a formal method than maintaining a consistent attitude toward the patient that creates an atmosphere of warmth, understanding, and dependability. In supportive therapy the therapist does not attempt to provide insights—although the patient may learn something about aspects of his behavior or its impact on others that he was not aware of before. The therapist may suggest, advise, or direct; but, in so doing, his primary aim is to help the patient re-establish his previously successful ways of coping with problems. Giving support encourages communication, first with the therapist and then with others in the patient's life.

Supportive therapy has much in common with the help provided by members of the clergy, thoughtful teachers who counsel students, and others whom Schofield (1964) has called the "invisible" therapists. These are men and women, he explains, who "by virtue of the roles they occupy and the status they hold as exemplars of stability, wisdom and devotion to service are regularly turned to for help by persons in need of counsel and emotional support." Attorneys and family physicians may also function in this way, depending on their sensitivity, maturity, and willingness to give time to such counseling, which Schofield calls "therapeutic conversation."

Why does supportive therapy work? There is no single theoretical explanation, just as there is no "school" of supportive psychotherapy. Although some research has thrown light on the conditions under which patients are likely to feel support from the therapist, there has been little research that helps explain why support is effective with so many people. Still, a theoretical basis for explaining the therapeutic effect of support may be found in research on infant behavior. The studies of Ribble (1944) and Spitz (1945) on human infants have made clear that close attention, handling, and physical contact are necessary for children to develop physically and emotionally. Their studies strongly suggest that very young children have a "contact hunger" that can be satisfied only through physical closeness. The studies of Bowlby (1969) indicate that the behavior of children which elicits contact is unlearned, or instinctive. His studies show that the need for closeness continues through childhood and, though it may diminish later, never disappears. He also found, not surprisingly, that when children are separated from their parents (who provided the closeness), they become upset and depressed, and that such depression could be alleviated by ending the separation.

As children grow older, their contact hunger is satisfied more and more by communication, and the need for physical contact (excluding sex) diminishes. Adults are likely to have most of their needs for closeness met through communication with their families, friends, or respected persons to whom they turn for help. Feeling understood seems to be an important element in such communication. In situations that provoke anxiety or depression, the need for close contact increases. When people turn to a psychotherapist for help, they are usually in such situations. If the therapist's manner is warm and communicates understanding, this provides the basis for an attachment, and the patient will experience a feeling of closeness. Schofield calls this "purchased friendship." One might also draw an analogy between the support a therapist gives a patient and the physical contact and soothing words a parent gives a frightened or depressed child.

In the next chapter we shall take up a briefer form of supportive therapy, crisis intervention.

REFERENCES

Bowlby, J. *Attachment and Loss, Vol. I. Attachment.* New York: Basic Books, 1969.

Enelow, A. J., and Wexler, M. *Psychiatry in the Practice of Medicine.* New York: Oxford University Press, 1966.

Kaiser, H. *Effective Psychotherapy*, ed. by L. B. Fierman. New York: Free Press, 1965.

Ribble, M. "Infantile Experience in Relation to Personality Development." In *Personality and the Behavior Disorders* II, ed. by J. McV. Hunt. New York: Ronald Press, 1944, pp. 621–51.

Rogers, C. R. "The Characteristics of a Helping Relationship." In *Contemporary Psychotherapies*, ed. by M. I. Stein. New York: Free Press of Glencoe, 2nd ed. 1962.

Schofield, W. *Psychotherapy: The Purchase of Friendship.* Englewood Cliffs, N.J.: Prentice-Hall, Inc., 1964.

Spitz, R. "Hospitalism, An Inquiry into the Genesis of Psychiatric Conditions in Early Childhood." In *Psychoanalytic Study of the Child* I. New York: International Universities Press, 1945, pp. 255–78.

7

CRISIS INTERVENTION

During the past twenty years, the term *crisis* has been appearing with increasing frequency in the mental health literature. Erickson (1959) introduced the term *developmental crisis* to describe normal periods of emotional upset as individuals mature and move from one stage of personal development to another, as from pre-adolescence to adolescence, or from young adulthood to middle age. Caplan (1964) introduced a crisis theory of brief psychotherapy. In his belief, psychotherapeutic intervention at a time of crisis could be a type of primary prevention of serious mental illness. He defined crisis intervention as the provision of appropriate supportive and counseling measures that help an individual cope with his response to a crisis, thereby lessening the possibility of more serious disturbance. Such crises are seen not as mental or emotional illness, in the sense of neurosis or psychosis, but as a loss of psychological equilibrium due to some psychological, biological, or social change that creates stress. As Caplan wrote in 1964:

> In his individual emotional functioning and his performance as a unit of the social structure, a person operates in certain consistent patterns with minimal self-awareness and sense of strain. He is constantly faced with situations calling for problem-solving ac-

tivity, and with minimal delay, he solves his problems by habitual mechanisms and reactions.

In Caplan's view, crises occur when people encounter difficulties that cannot be resolved readily by their usual problem-solving behavior. Failure to cope with those difficulties increases tension; anxiety, fear, and feelings of guilt or depression develop in accordance with the nature of the problem and with the person's habitual response to similar problems. If continued efforts to cope with the problem are unsuccessful, the individual's behavior may become increasingly disorganized and his psychological symptoms increasingly severe. On the other hand, a crisis can be a growth experience if the person responds by developing new problem-solving behavior that is both socially acceptable and realistic.

Whether the first or second outcome occurs will depend on such considerations as the individual's psychological strength, the presence or absence of family support, community attitudes toward the person and toward the type of problem he has, and the availability of professional help. Help in resolving a crisis can come from any quarter. This is because the necessary help is chiefly emotional support, supplemented ideally by counseling about feasible alternative ways of dealing with the problem. Such support and counseling—or crisis intervention—can be provided by a variety of professionals who use counseling or psychotherapy in their work, and by family members, friends, or other persons influential in the individual's social environment.

This view of crises and crisis intervention leads to a useful classification: *developmental crises* (sometimes referred to as maturational crises), which can occur at any point in life as one moves from one developmental stage to another; *situational crises*, resulting from external stress such as personal illness; *family crises*, occurring when the social support function of the family is disrupted by either internal stress from a family member or external stress on the family unit. All of these crises fit Caplan's description and call for somewhat similar supportive treatment.

In community mental health centers and the psychiatric services of general hospitals, however, a related but different application of crisis theory has developed. In such facilities the clients tend to be chronic psychiatric patients or to have severe neuroses or personality disturbances. Because of the increasing number of former mental hospital patients now treated in the community as outpatients, there is great pressure on community agencies to provide them with services—and these tend to be long-term. Many of such patients are receiving medication for chronic psychoses. The group includes a large number who are seen in the clinic only when they experience a *mental illness crisis*, or acute exacerbation of a chronic psychosis, often not easily classified as one of the three types of crises described above. Crisis intervention is usually defined more broadly now to include brief symptomatic treatment of such patients, and is aimed at restoring the previous equilibrium, or at partial remission of symptoms.

DEVELOPMENTAL CRISES

Almost everyone experiences new stresses and must cope with tension as he moves from one phase of his life to the next. Leaving home to begin daily attendance at school, entering adolescence, getting married, birth of the first child, and the onset of awareness of middle age and old age are classic times of stress. The fortunate ones are those who can turn to someone close to them for support at such times, or whose inner resources are sufficient to meet the challenge of new problems. When others fail to help, or a person lacks inner resources, he may come to a psychotherapist.

> Frank C., a 14-year-old, was the oldest son of a mathematics teacher. Frank's father was determined to motivate his son to have an academic career as a mathematician or scientist, and hoped to accomplish this by pushing Frank to study and by frequently testing Frank's knowledge of mathematics against his own. However, Frank's inclination was toward music rather than mathematics and science, where his aptitude was limited. He experienced the pressure as competition. As he entered adolescence

and became interested in girls and social activities with peers, he began to lose interest in school. He had difficulty concentrating and retaining what he had studied. After Frank had failed several examinations, his mother became sufficiently concerned to bring him to a psychotherapist. Frank accompanied her willingly.

A personable boy with an excellent vocabulary, Frank described his difficulty at the first interview as lack of interest in school. "I like fun, girls, and movies better than studying and school," he said. But he was aware that his failures were upsetting to his parents—which bothered him, and he was also losing confidence in himself, feeling discouraged, guilty, and at times depressed. "I can never be a scholar like my father, but I do need help so I can make passing grades, at least," he said. His mother made it clear that there was considerable tension in his relations with his father.

In several ensuing sessions with Frank, the therapist discussed this relationship with him. At first he encouraged Frank to describe the interchanges he had with his father. Doing so, Frank described his feelings that he could never be as scholarly, as good in mathematics, as his father. Through active questioning the therapist helped Frank identify his own interests and areas of strength. He then supported Frank in the legitimacy of having different life goals than those chosen by his father. The therapist also reassured Frank that his interest in girls and social events was normal and healthy. As Frank's confidence grew, his ability to concentrate returned, and his performance in school improved. In the fifth session Frank reported a conversation with his father, that went roughly as follows:

FRANK: So Dad began his usual quizzing and I told him that I didn't want to be tutored at home. I said I wasn't that interested in math anyway, and that dinnertime shouldn't be like school.

THERAPIST: Good for you! What happened then?

FRANK: Well, he was really surprised. He started to say something and Mom just said, "Edward!" and gave him her look—the one that says, "that's enough." He said, "I guess you're right, Son."

THERAPIST: That must have made you feel good.

FRANK: Yes, it did. I don't think he's going to stop bugging me about school, though.

THERAPIST: No. Probably not. But you can stand up for yourself and he'll respect you for it.

FRANK: I saw that last night.

After three more sessions, a total of eight, Frank and the therapist agreed that he could now cope with the problem himself. He could enjoy his new feelings and interests as an adolescent and still live comfortably with his more scholarly father.

This is an example of a crisis developing in very early adolescence when young people become interested in heterosexual involvements and social events with peers, often with a consequent reduction in interest in schoolwork. At that stage, too, young people begin to be aware of their own talents and inclinations, which are often different from those of their parents. This strengthening of their sense of personal identity is often conflict-laden, as it can distance them from their parents and create feelings of disloyalty, and they may not have anyone to turn to for support. In Frank's case, the exploration of his feelings, his areas of strength, and his differences from his father in addition to the support from the therapist enabled him to deal with the conflicts interfering with his ability to study. His father was able to accept, at least to a degree, Frank's assertion of independence, his rejection of his father's ambitions for him. Had he not, family interviews would then have been appropriate.

> After entering high school at fourteen, Sarah L. began to notice that when she was talking to a teacher or a young boy face to face, or when she had to recite in front of the class, or when she was at dances, she would suddenly feel warm and flushed, and others would comment that her skin had turned deep red. At such times her entire face and shoulder area reddened and her face felt very hot. The experience was very embarrassing to her, and yet she was not aware of any embarrassment leading to the flushing. She became sensitive about it and began to wear high-necked dresses or blouses.
>
> Sarah was a tall, well-developed young woman appearing somewhat older than fourteen. In therapy she talked freely and easily when asked questions or was encouraged to speak, but she could not initiate conversation with the therapist. As Sarah continued

to deny that she was uncomfortable, embarrassed, or worried about personal encounters or class performance, the therapist decided to use confrontation to clarify the situation. The following interchange took place:

THERAPIST: I find this rather puzzling. You tell me that there is nothing bothering you about boys or your performance in class, yet your symptoms all say you are embarrassed and unsure of yourself. It doesn't seem to fit.

SARAH: (*After a thoughtful pause*) Well, maybe I don't feel as good as I've been saying. I just hate to admit it to anybody.

THERAPIST: It sounds like that's the problem. You can't admit it to anybody, not even to yourself. But your skin gives you away.

SARAH: Well, I really have been worried and I don't think I'm doing as well as I should in school. And being with boys embarrasses me. I feel all kinds of things that I don't understand.

During the rest of the interview the therapist provided reassurance about the normalcy of all the difficulties being described, and they discussed the value of openly expressing feelings of discomfort of the sort that Sarah had been trying to disguise. Sarah's mother was then invited into the consulting room and was reassured in Sarah's presence that the problems were a normal part of development and that the "symptom" could not be considered an illness. The therapist suggested that Sarah try to be open with others about her discomfort or embarrassment, and that she could feel free to make an appointment to discuss the difficulties if they persisted. No further appointments were made.

About six months later Sarah phoned the therapist to thank him for his help and to inform him that the flushing had diminished to a tolerable level shortly after her interview, and that she had been admitting to herself and others when she felt embarrassed or ill at ease.

This type of case is sometimes mistakenly converted into a course of psychotherapy. Sarah was encountering the self-consciousness that many adolescents feel as they become acutely aware of sexual impulses and of the attention that adolescent boys and girls give each other and their physical features. The embarrassment of standing before the class and showing her new adult figure was a normal part of adolescent development for this somewhat insecure and unassertive girl, who was by no means suffering from a neurosis. Reassurance, gaining the confidence that comes with experience, and simple desensitization over time were probably the factors that helped Sarah through this benign developmental crisis.

Mary Jane H. was a 24-year-old married woman whose husband was an electrician in business for himself. The effort to build up his business kept him busy much of the time. He left early in the morning and returned very late at night six days a week. After Mrs. H. gave birth to her second child, she felt somewhat elated at first but soon became anxious and depressed. She had not had such feelings after the birth of the first child two years before. But now she found that there was more work than she had expected with the arrival of the second. Her life seemed to have become an endless round of taking care of babies. She grew bored, then lethargic and depressed. At times she even thought fleetingly of suicide. Concerned about the significance of these depressions, she visited her family doctor who referred her to a psychotherapist for consultation.

At the interview she was somewhat hyperactive, moving about the office and speaking rather rapidly. She stated that her feelings of depression were diminishing but that she was bored with routine housework and baby care and felt that too much of her life was being absorbed by these tasks. She was anxious about being a "good mother" and also about doing the "right thing" for her husband. Her main problem seemed to be a fear of the new responsibility brought on by the arrival of the second child at a time when her husband was increasingly involved in his growing business.

The therapist reassured her that her reaction was not abnormal and that her concerns were appropriate. He was supportive about her feelings of concern and her unhappiness at having to cope with the greater household responsibilities when her husband could offer her less assistance. At the conclusion of the interview Mrs. H. was told that she could return if she felt a need but should phone in a week. She did so and said that she felt fine. About three months later her physician informed the therapist that she had improved rapidly after the single session and that her symptoms had disappeared.

SITUATIONAL CRISES

Change is stressful. When changes in a person's life occur, such as a move to a new home, a new job with different responsibilities, economic changes, or unexpected illness, habitual modes of responding to one's social environment may no longer be appropriate. The necessity of coping with such changes, of dealing with different behavior from others, of new demands on oneself, and unexpected problems, can threaten an individual's sense of psychological or social integrity. In moderate degrees, heightened anxiety probably improves problem-solving ability but is nonetheless uncomfortable. In larger degrees, anxiety can be disorganizing. Among the life changes that usually create stress are death of a spouse, divorce, personal injury or illness, loss of a job, retirement, health crises in family members, and re-entry of family members from an earlier era with whom one still has unresolved conflicts.

When the individual encountering such an event finds that his usual problem-solving resources are insufficient to deal with it and that new solutions must be found, anxiety may mount to such a degree that the initial response is disorganized. Psychophysiologic symptoms such as neurodermatitis or headaches may appear, or a chronic disease may flare up. There is a growing body of evidence that in times of stress people are more susceptible to illness of all types. In one study, for example, major life changes were shown to be followed by illnesses of significant degree within the next year in a very high proportion of the individuals in the group studied (Rahe, 1972).

> R.D., a 35-year-old physicist, had had a period of dermatitis while completing his Ph.D. dissertation and preparing for the oral examination. The skin condition cleared up rapidly after he successfully completed the work and was awarded his degree. He then took a position as an instructor in the physics department at a state college. He did fine work and was praised for some of his research contributions. After presenting a paper at a major con-

ference, he was offered a position as a research physicist with a large, well-endowed laboratory. When he began his new job, he discovered that he was to be in charge of a laboratory with technicians and younger scientists (close to his own age) under his supervision. Once again his skin lesion appeared. He became upset about it, and found the itching almost intolerable.

Mr. D. was a quiet, self-effacing man with an apologetic manner, who had difficulty speaking out. After four weekly interviews, during which he was given the opportunity to talk about his feelings and was encouraged to express his concern about his new responsibilities, the dermatitis disappeared.

H.F. was a 45-year-old man who had always been rather passive and compliant, and tried to be a "good employee" in his work as a sales clerk. When economic reverses in his employer's business led to his dismissal, he became depressed, anxious, and sexually impotent. He feared he was losing his self-confidence to such a degree that he would never be able to work again. The therapist listened to the description of his difficulties, then said something like, "I can see what's happening. Losing your job has made you lose confidence in yourself in all areas, including sex. This cycle of fear is feeding on itself. You must stop surrendering to your fears and get out and find yourself a job. If you can begin working again you will see you are still capable of doing something worthwhile."

This directive approach was successful. Mr. F. returned once more, two weeks later, to announce that he had a job and felt better already. Several months later he phoned to say that his symptoms were gone.

Mrs. A.F. was a 63-year-old widow who had been depressed since the death of her husband about six months before the interview. Her main problem was fear of making decisions and a sense of being incomplete. She was sad and ruminated constantly about her husband and the many things that they had done together.

After three sessions during which she was encouraged to talk about her husband, her feelings about his loss, and the way she had been able to function before his death, she felt better. Although the therapist was supportive throughout these interviews, he gave no advice or direction, as he saw that she was coming to conclusions without it.

These are three simple but characteristic examples of situational crises. In the first case the patient was functioning well, but the stressful new situation had had a psychophysiological effect—his dermatitis. Since he was the kind of person who does not permit himself to think about personal problems or face his feelings, the therapist's work was facilitative, encouraging expression of feelings, and supportive. In the second case a man was paralyzed by mounting fear when a stressful event—the loss of his job—dealt a severe blow to his tenuous self-confidence. In that case the therapist was directive, using his authority as therapist to "push" the patient into doing something calculated to restore his self-confidence. The third patient, grieving, needed only support in order to be able to complete the mourning process and loosen her ties to her deceased husband.

FAMILY CRISES

In our society the family is no longer so strong or so stable a unit as it once was. In general, it has fewer members and a lesser economic function. In times of crisis there is less immediate help available, less support for decision making. Nevertheless, a chief function of the family is still (and perhaps even more importantly now) the provision of emotional support to its members. Because family members tend to depend strongly on each other for such support, and because other social ties are often weak, families are vulnerable to stress, and a crisis in a family affects all its members.

Hill (1965) described the family as "an arena of interacting personalities." In his formulation, when the blame for stress can be placed outside the family, the event may bring together rather than disorganize a family; but when the stress originates within the family (e.g., in illegitimacy, mental breakdown, infidelity, suicide, alcoholism), it is much more disruptive. When stress occurs, the family must often reorganize itself. Roles and responsibilities may have to be redefined. When one of the family members is the source of stress, the problem is present constantly and its effect tends to be divisive, reducing the family's ability to reassign roles and "take up the slack."

A family crisis may also be precipitated by one member who behaves in an unacceptable way to bring out into the open a chronic disturbance in the family. When this happens, the apparent personal crisis, upon examination, can be seen clearly as a family crisis that has been brought on by an effort to escape—or possibly to help resolve the long-standing family problem.

John S., a 16-year-old high school student, was referred by a pediatrician after having announced to his father that he was addicted to heroin. His father, quite agitated, phoned the pediatrician, who immediately contacted the therapist, who thereupon arranged for hospitalization. When seen at the hospital, John was remarkably calm, though rather sullen. He spoke fluently and showed signs neither of drug intoxication nor of withdrawal. His story sounded fantastic and was obviously invented. He wished to be sent to a Public Health Service hospital in San Antonio, Texas, for detoxification. When confronted with obvious inconsistencies in his story, John admitted that he was not addicted to heroin at all and that he wanted to move to San Antonio to live with his grandparents. He was having difficulty studying, and consequently trouble in school, because he was upset over the incessant arguing of his parents. He was frightened of his father's explosive temper, which was often vented at him or his mother. He longed for the relative peace and quiet of his grandparents' home.

John was discharged from the hospital at once. A conference was arranged with him and his parents the next day. The parents admitted that their marriage was an unhappy one, that the atmosphere at home was stormy, and they agreed to begin marital counseling. As the counseling progressed, the stormy scenes at home diminished and John was able to re-establish good study habits.

When a family member becomes mentally ill, a severe family crisis usually develops. The behavior of the disturbed family member is likely to be disruptive, sometimes because of its unpredictability. The necessity to take action troubles all family members. Calling in professional help or arranging for hospitalization can create guilt feelings. Tension arises when family members disagree about the appropriate steps to take, or whether any should be taken.

> Mildred P. was a 56-year-old married woman with two grown children, both living nearby. After her children had grown up, left home, and established families of their own, she took a part-time position as a clerk to fill her time and provide additional family income. This upset her husband, who had always been a rather possessive man. He began to follow her movements very closely, timing her absences from home for such things as grocery shopping, and checking on the interval between her departure from home and her arrival at work. He made accusations about possible infidelity, and began to behave in a threatening way about her "unexplained" periods of travel between destinations. But in the presence of their children he behaved quite reasonably, and this made Mrs. P. wonder if she was mistaken, despite her certainty that there was no basis for his suspicions about the time she spent on household errands or going to work. Finally convinced that her husband was paranoid, Mrs. P. had difficulty persuading family members and close friends with whom she talked. After he threatened physical violence, she spoke to her family doctor, who arranged for a family interview with the therapist.
>
> At the beginning of the interview, Mr. P. was reasonable and calm. But as different family members questioned him more closely, his calmness changed to anger. Finally he burst out with accusations of sexual infidelity on the part of his wife. It was then clear to all members of the family that Mr. P. was psychologically disturbed. When one of his daughters stated that her mother had been with her on one of the occasions of suspected infidelity, Mr. P. turned on her and angrily accused her of collusion. Once aware of each other's support, the family members were able to take steps to arrange for treatment for Mr. P.

Serious physical illness may also lead to family crisis. And when the illness is prolonged, major problems of adjustment are posed, not only for the patient but for family members as well (Kaplan et al., 1973). Open communication about the illness and its prognosis, and the affirmation of mutual support between members, help families cope with such situations.

MENTAL ILLNESS CRISES

By far the most common application of this type of crisis intervention is found in community mental health centers. Intervention to deal with the crises that occur during the course of psychotic illnesses differs from other types of crisis intervention in at least one important way. With the large population of patients who periodically become clients of the mental health care system, intervention efforts are classified as secondary prevention, rather than primary. That is, the aim of such crisis intervention is to prevent long stays in inpatient facilities, and further social disability, rather than to prevent mental illness. The provision of support, counseling with situational problems, antipsychotic medication, counseling with family members, brief stays in the structured environment of the inpatient ward, and early transfer to transitional facilities such as day treatment centers, therapeutic communities, or halfway houses, can reduce sharply the duration of inpatient care. Perhaps more importantly, these measures help prevent development of the dependence on a structured hospital environment formerly considered a symptom of mental illness. By reinforcing the patient's strengths and ability to remain independent, and by returning him quickly to as close an approximation to community living as he can tolerate, they deny the patient an opportunity to settle into passive acceptance of institutionalization, with its requirement of conformity to routines established for the staff's convenience and efficiency.

Mental illness crisis intervention is best accomplished in a system of facilities organized around the philosophy just described. A 24-hour-a-day emergency clinic available to the entire community and fully staffed with a multidisciplinary mental health team is the first requirement. The clinic must have available at all times inpatient beds for short-stay patients. There must also be a variety of treatment facilities with different degrees of structure or supervision of patients. These might include an open but supervised residential setting with a 24-hour-a-day program; an open setting with an evening program, or halfway house; an all-day therapeutic program without evening and night care; and a more conventional outpatient clinic that can accept patients without an intervening period on a "waiting list." These need not all be housed in the same place or administered by the same organization. There must, however, be a well-defined communication system connecting them, and the transfer of patients between them must be easy to accomplish. Access to other resources is also necessary.

It would go beyond the scope of this book to describe the organizational issues in the design and maintenance of such a network of services. We can, however, indicate the several functions the therapist in such a situation has to fulfill. Rosenbaum and Beebe (1975) stress that in psychiatric emergencies the crisis therapist is most effective when he defines himself as a consultant. He listens for a theme in what the patient is saying in order to decide on a strategy—usually a referral. Being familiar with the options, he discusses the relevant ones with the patient. Having arrived at a decision with which the patient can agree, the therapist must follow through, making certain that the patient knows where he is going, why, and how he will get there.

Thus, the intervention begins with data gathering. Giving support when it is needed will be especially facilitative if a patient is acutely disturbed. Having facilitated a patient's expression of feeling, the therapist will usually hear a great deal about his problems. His main task is then to make a social diagnosis. That is, rather than attempting to determine the diagnostic nomenclature that best fits the patient's disturbed behavior, he should look for clues to the social breakdown that has occurred. How was the patient functioning before the crisis? What were his sources of social support? What happened to upset the equilibrium that preceded the present crisis? What is the best way to provide social support (i.e., the well-structured environment of a hospital ward, or the less structured day treatment center) until the old equilibrium can be restored or a new one established? To get this information it is useful to interview family or friends of the patient as well—though many patients suffering acute exacerbations of chronic illness, such as those already living in a partial care facility, may have no one close to them. When there are significant others, they should be present during discussion of a treatment strategy.

The crisis intervention continues in the setting chosen for the patient by the clinic staff. Now, however, the care is likely to be a team effort. One staff member is usually designated as primary therapist and becomes the patient's advocate, helping him cope with the policies, procedures, constraints, and troublesome aspects of the treatment setting or the people in it. He offers support, helps interpret reality to the patient, and is firm from the outset in directing the patient's attention toward participating in making plans for discharge and placement thereafter.

When the patient can take part in discharge planning, he should be ready to leave the hospital for a less-structured setting. The decision is always based on observable behavioral change in the patient, not on abatement of a thought disorder, delusional ideas, or hallucinations. In other words, the schizophrenic patient, e.g., may be no less *psychologically* aberrant at the point of readiness for discharge than he was on admission. He should, however, be less aberrant *socially*. He should now be capable of adjustment to a less tightly structured environment. He should need much less supervision in order to remain undisturbed and undisturbing to others and to avoid self-destructive behavior.

Julia H., a 35-year-old married woman with two children, had been placed in a psychiatric hospital for the first time at age 25. At that time she had been suspicious, withdrawn, uncommunicative, and extremely fearful, becoming violently combative when anyone approached her. After several months in the hospital, she was discharged on phenothiazine medication with outpatient follow-up. After the birth of her second child nine years later, she became acutely depressed, uncommunicative, suspicious, angry, and withdrawn at times, as in the previous psychotic episode. She was hospitalized for a brief period and then discharged with medication and outpatient visits. Several weeks later she took 75 phenothiazine tablets from a new prescription that she had just received.

After acute medical detoxification she was interviewed in the emergency clinic. Mrs. H.'s appearance was that of a rather overweight woman with a remarkably blank facial expression. She was quite uncommunicative at first. When asked about her difficulties, her response was guarded and noncommital. The interviewer asked, "Why were you brought to the clinic?" Mrs. H. replied, "They must be afraid I'll do it again." "And are you considering it?" "I really would rather not say." The interview continued in this unproductive way. The patient's husband was invited into the office and asked for his account of the recent events. His manner was one of concern, confusion, and apparent helplessness as he described the patient's history in some detail. As he spoke, the patient became more communicative, primarily expressing anger and suspiciousness toward her husband. And as she became angrier toward her husband, she became friendlier toward the interviewer. Now she behaved as though her husband had failed her, while the interviewer apparently had become a new-found ally.

Arrangements were quickly made for outpatient follow-up, beginning with a brief period of treatment at a day treatment center the patient was functioning as well as she had before this most recent breakdown. She was followed subsequently for two years while day care was arranged for her children. Within six weeks, through monthly interviews and remained essentially asymptomatic.

Under ideal circumstances, mental illness crisis intervention is followed by social rehabilitation, the aim of which is to reduce the likelihood of another crisis. In Chapter 8, some typical social rehabilitation methods are discussed.

REFERENCES

Caplan, Gerald. *Principles of Preventive Psychiatry*. New York: Basic Books, 1964.
Erickson, E. H. "Identity and the Life Cycle." In *Psychological Issues*

Monographs. 1:1. New York: International Universities Press, 1959.

Hill, Reuben. "Generic Features of Families under Stress." In *Crisis Intervention: Selected Readings,* ed. by H. J. Parad, New York: Family Service Association, 1965.

Kaplan, David M.; Smith, Aaron; Grobstein, Rose; and Fischman, S. E. "Family Mediation of Stress." *Social Work* 18:60–69, 1973.

Rahe, R. H. "Subjects' Recent Life Changes and Their Near-Future Illness Reports." *Annals of Clinical Research* 4:250–65, 1972.

Rosenbaum, C. P., and Beebe, J. E. *Psychiatric Treatment: Crisis, Clinic and Consultation.* New York: McGraw-Hill, 1975.

8

SOCIAL REHABILITATION

The approaches to psychotherapy described in preceding chapters are probably applicable largely to persons with neurotic, psychosomatic, or personality disorders who voluntarily seek treatment. They are not generally used with chronically psychotic patients who may often require periods of hospitalization.

With the development of community mental health centers, an increasingly great number of patients who suffer from chronic psychotic disorders have entered the mental health care system for outpatient treatment. This is a consequence of the wide use, since the middle 1950s, of phenothiazine drugs for the treatment of psychoses. Control of psychotic symptoms by these chemical agents has resulted in the rapid discharge of large numbers of patients from state hospitals after some had spent many years there. Indeed, nowadays far fewer psychiatric patients are even committed to a long-term inpatient treatment facility. Psychotherapy in community facilities has made it possible to give much shorter periods of inpatient treatment followed by outpatient care.

Follow-up care for patients discharged from mental hospitals was first provided through state-operated after-care clinics, which were common in the 1950s. These have been largely replaced by

community mental health centers, which provide crisis intervention, outpatient treatment, and brief inpatient treatment, in addition to aftercare for former inpatients. These facilities also provide
outpatient group and individual therapy for chronically ill psychiatric patients who can remain in the community.

Out of more than twenty years of experience with such chroni-
cally-ill psychiatric patients in community mental health centers, a
social rehabilitation model of outpatient care has evolved. This
approach to psychotherapy developed from the simple reassurance,
supportive care, and checking of the medication dosages and their
side effects obtaining in the earlier after-care clinics; but its goals,
of course, are more ambitious than simply "maintenance" through
medication and psychological support. Since the social rehabilitation model is primarily addressed not to psychological or cognitive
factors but rather to social behavior, the term "rehabilitation" is
more appropriate than "psychotherapy."

Social rehabilitation therapy is based on the fact that most
chronically psychotic patients have lost important skills of social
adaptation that are commonplace among non-psychotic persons.
This may be due to the illness itself or to a long stay in a mental
hospital where opportunities to exercise such skills are scarce. Or it
may be related to the patient's efforts to cope with the response of
others to his psychotic behavior. Whatever the cause, however, the
treatment team makes little effort to identify it. They concentrate
instead on teaching patients the everyday social skills needed for
community life by providing practical information, models to emu-
late, and social support. The skills taught include how to get from
one place to another via the public transportation system; how to
shop for groceries and prepare appropriate and nutritious meals;
and how to obtain and disburse wisely the small amounts of income that may be available to them.

The problem of social isolation is common among psychotic patients. Their behavior usually is unacceptable to non-psychotics.
Thus there may be no place for them other than the mental health

care system. Most psychotic persons also bear the onus attached to accepting "welfare" payments or living on some other type of public support. This explains why provision of the social support needed for reasonable psychological comfort is another goal of social rehabilitation.

TYPES OF SOCIAL REHABILITATION

Two typical kinds of social rehabilitation therapy are day treatment programs in which patients receive treatment through much of the day but spend the night at home, and transitional residential programs that provide, in a non-hospital setting, evening and night care, or sometimes 24-hour care, in addition to day activities. For patients who are deeply regressed and withdrawn, simple supportive group meetings affording opportunity for some communication with others may also be organized, even though they may not be able to take part in activities with more ambitious goals.

Among the characteristics of a social rehabilitation program are:

1. Strong emphasis on group activities.
2. Individual and group counseling focused on helping the patient become more adaptive and self-sufficient, rather than accepting a disabled status. Sometimes group counseling aims also to help patients learn to discuss with others their needs or feelings or distress.
3. Discussions oriented toward problems of everyday life like those involved in obtaining and preparing food, in self-care, traveling, and providing clothing and housing for oneself. Whenever possible, these programs aim to develop skills to make the patients employable.

Social rehabilitation is action- or activity-oriented. When problems are discussed, they tend to be external rather than intrapsychic. A group is more likely to be engaged in a task or activity or discussion of the activity than in a discussion of the sources of their problems. The group is given a great deal of responsibility for deciding which activities are to be undertaken. In many programs a "patient government" sets the group's rules, including those for dealing with such problems as non-participation and disruptive behavior. Behaving in a contributory and non-disruptive way is rewarded by the approbation of the staff and of those patients who are also capable of such behavior. Discussions of tensions that arise in the group are encouraged.

Outpatient social rehabilitation

Rada and his colleagues (1969) have described an eight-year experience with a type of outpatient social rehabilitation that they called "adaptive psychotherapy." This approach involves (1) patient contact over an extended, sometimes indefinite, period of time; (2) contacts generally for less than 25 minutes and less often than weekly; (3) frequent use of psychotropic drugs; (4) goals that are varied but not aimed primarily at insight, transference exploration, or interpretation; (5) techniques that include support, suppression, an institutional alliance, advice, environmental manipulation, attention to life happenings, and promotion of accurate assessments of the real world surrounding the patient.

The concept of an institutional alliance has been presented under a variety of labels by other authors. It involves the fact that patients feel a sense of continuity of care that is a function of their connection with an institution (clinic or mental health center). Although therapist personnel will probably change—since the patient is likely to be in a program for a long time—this institutional alliance will endure. That is, as long as the principles of therapy remain the same. Patients who are capable of social functioning at a better than marginal level with support are appropriate for outpatient therapy. This may follow a period in a day treatment center, which is for the very marginally adjusted patient or for gradual reintroduction to the community after hospital treatment.

Social rehabilitation in the hospital

When psychiatric patients are hospitalized, it is usually because they have become distressed to the point of panic, and their behavior is disturbing to others around them. While some patients are relieved to be admitted to a hospital, whose physical confines and social structure can offer a sense of security, many are frightened by the institution and all that it stands for. The first task of the therapist, therefore, is to be supportive while communicating a sense of stability and reliability to the patient. Usually disorganized, patients may also behave bizarrely or be hostile or compliant or withdrawn and uncommunicative. Almost always they need the reassurance that can be communicated by a competent and friendly therapist. Accordingly, the therapist's behavior is the most important element of such inpatient psychotherapy.

The ward atmosphere itself is also important. The term *milieu therapy* refers to the use of ward atmosphere, attitudes of the staff, and relations between all staff and patients (and between the patients themselves) as therapy. A therapeutic ward milieu depends to a large extent on open communication among staff members and between staff and patients, and, of course, on good morale among the staff. Activities, a secondary part of milieu therapy, offer patients opportunities to engage in rewarding social experiences, to practice problem solving and decision making, to take increasing responsibility for their own actions, and to make the transition to a less-structured environment. In general, the individual and group activities and the staff's attitudes toward patients should convey positive, optimistic expectations about the patients' potential for return to a more self-sufficient and non-institutional life.

Although the concept of milieu therapy is very old, its application to hospital treatment began to spread widely after World War II. As programs evolved from custodial care to planned efforts to promote therapeutic interactions between staff and patients, the idea that a hospital could be a "therapeutic community" emerged (Jones, 1953). Efforts were made to plan patient activities around

therapeutic or rehabilitation goals, rather than simply to keep patients busy. Increasing their participation in decision making, both
for themselves and for the group, became a goal. The ultimate objective of self-sufficiency and adaptive social behavior became the
guiding principle.

In this social context the therapist can help the patient most by
offering a firm, supportive relation characterized by clear and un-
ambiguous communication. The simplest approach to the patient
is best: introducing oneself, describing the nature and frequency of
the interviews, and helping the patient make some sense out of
what is happening. Inferential conclusions about the patient's behavior or feelings should be avoided. Interviews should be relatively
frequent but need not be of uniform duration. They can range
from a few minutes to as much as an hour or more if the patient
has something he wishes to talk about. An important tactic for the
therapist is to clarify what the patient is trying to say when his
meaning is not clear by indicating this without attempting to interpret his statements. Another important focus for discussion
should be the patient's response to hospitalization as well as his
feelings in the period leading up to it. Still another of the therapist's aims should be to encourage the patient to make realistic
plans for discharge. Minimizing the length of stay in the hospital
should always be a goal of social rehabilitation. To these ends, appropriate medication, the ward milieu and activities, and the group
discussions will enhance the therapist's efforts.

> Mrs. N.M., a 30-year-old married woman, consulted the psycho-
> therapist because of depression. In the first interview it became
> apparent that the "depressions" she described were episodes of
> marked withdrawal. One of these episodes had resulted in a pe-
> riod of hospitalization in another part of the country about two
> years before. When asked to describe her feelings during the "de-
> pressions," she said that when talking with someone she would
> suddenly have a feeling of emptiness and great distance from the
> person. This feeling might last a few minutes or several days. She
> also reported vivid and frightening dreams, as of being boiled

alive, from which she would awaken in panic. Occasionally, Mrs. M. disappeared from her family for several days, telling no one where she had gone. At such times she moved from one place to another, checking in and out of motels, fearful that she was being followed. She often became preoccupied with the hidden meanings of gestures or remarks made by others, looking for threats to her life. Several days after the first interview, she phoned the therapist to say that someone might kill her. Immediate hospitalization, to which she willingly assented, was arranged.

In the hospital, phenothiazine medication was started at once. Mrs. M. was seen daily by the therapist. She attended group meetings, but said nothing. Later she reported that she could not trust anyone at first, so did not speak. As she became less fearful of staff and patients, she began to be more active in group discussions and ward projects. Each day the therapist devoted some time to encouraging her to discuss her feelings about the way the other patients and the staff behaved toward her, and Mrs. M. began to doubt her original interpretations of their words and gestures. The consistent and supportive behavior of staff and therapist helped in this regard.

After five days, plans were made for her return home and transfer to a day treatment center for continuing milieu therapy during the day. Her husband visited her on the ward, and the next day she left the ward to visit her two children and her husband. Then for the first time she mentioned the argument with her husband that had led to her sudden departure from home and frantic telephone call to the therapist. He had wanted her to entertain his family and became angry when she refused. The sudden feeling of emptiness and distance that was her customary response to anxiety recurred; she became fearful that he would kill her, and then fled. Now she could recognize that her response had been inappropriate. She was discharged on the eighth hospital day, to continue with outpatient therapy at the day treatment center and weekly sessions with her therapist.

SOCIAL REHABILITATION IN THE DAY TREATMENT CENTER

Day treatment centers usually represent a step between full hospitalization and the patient's return to full-time life in the commu-

nity. The milieu is still an important part of the treatment. Patients
are usually given a much larger role in both therapeutic and administrative decisions affecting them than in acute-care psychiatric
hospitals or wards. Typically, many activity and discussion groups
are available to patients. Goals set for the patients include increased responsibility for their own activities within the center;
increased ability to talk about interpersonal conflicts in group
meetings and to control impulsive actions in response to the conflicts; and active participation in vocational training.

Patients usually spend from three to six months in day treatment
center programs. Some then continue with regular outpatient therapy sessions from two to four times a month; others have irregular
outpatient follow-up sessions scheduled as needed.

As is generally held by mental health professionals working with
chronically psychotic patients, a day treatment center program is
less likely to produce regression and lowering of self-esteem than
is hospitalization. Thus, when a patient can be placed in such a
program instead of a hospital, it is preferable to do so. The availability of a day treatment center program permits earlier discharge
of patients from a psychiatric hospital. This means that social and
vocational roles at home and in the community can be resumed
much more quickly, family ties can be more easily maintained, and
permanent estrangement from family and other social groups outside the hospital is less likely to occur.

Day treatment centers were used as early as 1937 because of
shortages of inpatient beds (Herz, 1975). Their development was
given great impetus by the Community Mental Health Centers
Act of 1963, which specified that day hospitalization was a necessary component of a federally funded community mental health
center. The therapeutic community approach, with its emphasis on
sharing of decision making between patients and staff, proved very
appropriate for the day hospital setting. The studies of Herz and
his co-workers (1971) showed that patients treated at a day care
center from the beginning of therapy or after a brief period of hospitalization were less likely to be admitted, or re-admitted, to a psy-

chiatric hospital than those who received the same milieu therapy on an inpatient unit.

In a day treatment center, therapy is carried out chiefly in group activities; meanwhile the individual therapist (who is sometimes called a coordinator or primary therapist) talks with patients about day-to-day problems and social responsibilities in the center and helps them choose activities geared to eventual discharge. As the discharge date approaches, the focus of the talks usually shifts to job placement, vocational training, or other plans for resuming a more self-sufficient life in the community.

Characteristic day treatment center activities include arts and crafts; body movement, dance, and exercise groups; training in carpentry and other vocational or household skills; music; creative writing; discussion groups; psychodrama and role-playing of social-conflict situations. Group discussions may be oriented around specific problems, such as shyness, social isolation, or racial conflict. Or they may center on the governing of the patient community or such activities as operating a "coffee house" for the patients or organizing a garage sale. Some groups are organized for the discussion of current events and issues to help patients get in touch with the social and political concerns of the outside world. In all group activities efforts are made to foster the development of social skills by the patients.

> At the day treatment center Mrs. M. was most interested in the arts and crafts group. She took part, though at first only in individual projects. Then she joined some of the discussion groups that organized group activities. She avoided all groups that dealt with personal problems. With the help of the staff, she began to take some responsibility for organizing projects to be operated by the patients. During her weekly sessions with the therapist, she talked about her activities at the center, her art work, and, with the passage of time, her plans for resuming a more active role with her husband and family. Her artistic talent was such that the vocational rehabilitation counselor at the center encouraged her to enroll in design school. Mrs. M. was discharged from the center, to continue with outpatient therapy.

OUTPATIENT SOCIAL REHABILITATION

After patients have been discharged from an inpatient psychiatric unit or a day treatment center, they usually require continued care as an outpatient. This may have a regular weekly or twice-weekly schedule, or sessions may be scheduled irregularly at the patient's initiation. Duration of the sessions is often twenty to twenty-five minutes rather than the traditional forty-five to fifty minutes. The supportive approach described in Chapter 6 is usually appropriate for social rehabilitation, with a shift in emphasis toward the patient's problems in maintaining a non-institutional life. The therapist tries to direct the patient's attention away from delusional ideas or preoccupations, while encouraging work and social activities that lead to some degree of satisfaction.

After discharge from the center, Mrs. M. was seen at first at weekly intervals. The sessions focused on realistic problems and upsetting events in the period since the preceding appointment. Since most of Mrs. M.'s withdrawal episodes were provoked by a disturbing discussion with her husband, the therapist encouraged her to talk about these incidents. He discouraged discussion of her delusional ideas, or fears of harm, by redirecting her attention to the actual events that upset her. He also encouraged her to talk about interactions in general with her husband, her children, and anyone else with whom she came in contact.

After several months the periods of withdrawal diminished, and Mrs. M. stopped expressing delusional ideas, talking instead about her husband and family. In general, although she was still easily frightened by the anger of others she could control her impulses to run away. Her work in interior design was not only a creative outlet; it also reduced the intensity of her relations with family members and of their demands on her, which she had always found taxing. After six months, sessions were scheduled less frequently, and after about a year the appointments were made at Mrs. M.'s initiative. Whereas earlier she became delusional and retreated from social relations when faced with a problem, now she would make an appointment to see her therapist. This relation lasted for several years, during which Mrs. M. was successfully operating an interior design studio and functioning with an acceptable degree of effectiveness at home.

Social rehabilitation is an approach to the therapy of the chronically mentally ill that emphasizes learning or re-acquiring skills or social adaptation. Its goals are self-sufficiency and community living. It usually involves periods of treatment in inpatient units, day treatment centers, and outpatient settings, with consistent therapy in each setting as exemplified in the case of Mrs. M.

REFERENCES

Herz, M. I. "Partial Hospitalization: Day and Night Care." In *Comprehensive Textbook of Psychiatry II*, by A. Freedman, H. I. Kaplan, and B. J. Sadock, Baltimore: Williams and Wilkins, 1975.

Herz, M. I.; Endicott, J.; Spitzer, R. L.; and Mesnikoff, A. "Day vs. Inpatient Hospitalization: A Controlled Study." *American Journal of Psychiatry* 127:1371–82, 1971.

Jones, M. *The Therapeutic Community*. New York: Basic Books, 1963.

Rada, R. T.; Daniels, R. S.; and Draper, E. "An Outpatient Setting for Treating Chronically Ill Psychiatric Patients." *American Journal of Psychiatry* 126:789–95, 1969.

9

BEHAVIOR THERAPY
Michael L. Russell, Ph.D.

Behavior therapy is a relatively recent development in the psychiatric care of patients. It has arisen primarily from the efforts of clinicians and researchers to incorporate into psychiatric treatment the contributions of experimental psychology toward the understanding of human functioning. While the philosophical roots of behaviorism can be traced to the work of physicians and psychologists in the late 1800s and early 1900s, only during the past fifteen years has behavior therapy become a major influence in psychotherapy. The current status of behavior therapy within psychiatry has been characterized thus in an American Psychiatric Association Task Force Report (1973):

> Behavior therapy and behavioral principles employed in the analysis of clinical phenomena have reached a stage of development where they now unquestionably have much to offer informed clinicians in the service of modern and social psychiatry.

THE BEHAVIORAL APPROACH
The feature of behavior therapy that distinguishes it from other forms of psychotherapy is its focus on the patient's actions and in-

teractions within his current environment. In behavior therapy a
patient's psychiatric or psychological problem is regarded as a problem of behavior. That is, the patient's current behavior is viewed
as being in some manner inappropriate for his family, social group,
vocational setting, or individual situation, with the result that the
patient is in distress. For example, a patient's behavior could be
considered a problem if it occurs in an inappropriate place (e.g.,
exhibitionism), if it occurs too often (e.g., alcoholism or obesity),
if it does not occur often enough (e.g., sexual dysfunction), if it is
of inappropriate strength (e.g., fear or anxiety), or if it does not
occur at all (e.g., lack of social skills).

The task of the behavior therapist is to help the patient change
his current inappropriate behaviors and ensure the maintenance of
desirable behavior patterns. This usually involves the direct modification of the patient's life style in order that inappropriate behaviors are eliminated or reduced, desirable behaviors occur more frequently, and new appropriate behaviors are learned. Frequently the
patient's social and physical environment is also restructured to
support the patient's new appropriate actions and to discourage the
patient's undesirable behaviors. While a patient may initially present numerous problem behaviors, the therapist examines each behavior in turn and designs an intervention strategy for it.

UNDERSTANDING PROBLEM BEHAVIOR

As in every type of psychotherapy, the behavior therapist begins
by establishing rapport with the patient. In this phase of treatment
the therapist spends considerable time listening to the patient,
providing a supportive atmosphere, and gradually building up a
therapeutic relation. Using an open-ended interviewing style, the
behavior therapist encourages the patient to express his feelings
and concerns (see Chapter 2).

Once rapport exists, the therapist begins to focus on the patient's
problem behaviors. Initially the therapist obtains a thorough description of the patient's actions and interactions within his envi-

ronment. He attempts to identify the patient's behavioral excesses, deficits, and assets in order to answer such questions as: What specifically does the patient do that is inappropriate? Why is the behavior undesirable? When does the problem behavior occur? This *behavior profile* provides the therapist with a clear description of the characteristics of the problem behavior. Subsequent observations can be compared with this profile to assess the effects of treatment.

The therapist creates a behavior profile after examining each of the patient's problem behaviors in isolation from its social context. He determines the frequency, duration, and intensity of the behaviors. He seeks a measure of how often the behavior occurs (e.g., number of times per day), a measure of how long the behavior exists (e.g., number of minutes per occurrence), and a physical measure reflecting the severity of the behavior (e.g., closest distance the patient will come to a feared object). In a similar way, the therapist also identifies and examines the patient's appropriate behaviors upon which intervention strategies can be based.

To collect this information the therapist frequently asks the patient to keep a diary of what he does throughout the day, noting his thoughts and feelings at the time. If indicated, the therapist may even observe the patient in an actual problem situation to identify the problem behaviors firsthand.

The following case illustrates the process of obtaining a behavior profile:

> Mr. G., a 41-year-old research scientist in electrical engineering, sought treatment because of his feelings of low self-worth and dissatisfaction with his current life style. He stated that he was seeking "peace of mind."
>
> In the initial interview, Mr. G. described his concerns about his interpersonal relations and his difficulties in his current job. Slowly it emerged that Mr. G. was experiencing considerable anxiety over the possibility of being viewed by other people as "incompetent" or "ignorant." He had attempted to find relief from these feelings on his own by reading popular psychology books and practicing meditation, but without success.

The therapist first sought to elicit from Mr. G. the specific anxious feelings and thoughts that he was experiencing. For this purpose it was requested that Mr. G. keep a daily log of his activities, noting his moods and thoughts. During the next two sessions the therapist reviewed the log with Mr. G. and developed a behavior profile. Two types of problems were identified: 1. Mr. G.'s self-critical thoughts, and 2. his anxious feelings. In a social situation either at home or at work he often had the following thoughts: "This person knows more than I do. I don't know anything about this. He must think I'm stupid." In these interactions Mr. G. experienced extreme anxiety and exhibited a variety of nervous mannerisms (i.e., not looking at the other person, talking rapidly). Such interactions occurred two to four times a day, and Mr. G. felt anxious during each. He also became anxious if he perceived that a social interaction could occur, i.e., when he was sitting at his desk at work with his door open and a colleague walked down the hall. This happened five to ten times a day, and the anxious feelings and self-critical thoughts continued until he shut himself off from the possibility of interaction.

While the therapist is creating a profile of the patient's behavior, he is also gathering information needed for a *functional analysis* of the problem-behavior patterns. The purpose of this analysis is to determine how the patient's behavior fits into the surrounding social and physical environment; that is, the therapist attempts to identify the events affecting the patient's actions, as well as the effects of his actions on others. This information is used by the therapist to design a treatment strategy to change the patient's behavior and to predict the likely effects of his behavior changes on his environment. The therapist seeks to answer such questions as: How does the problem behavior operate to the advantage of the patient? How are people or events in his immediate environment precipitating and supporting the inappropriate behavior? What is preventing the desirable behavior from occurring?

In performing a functional analysis the therapist essentially pursues two kinds of information: (1) antecedents of the behavior—i.e., the events preceding the behavior, and (2) consequences of the behavior—i.e., the events following the behavior. Each type of information is important for understanding the problem-behavior pattern and, ultimately, for designing an effective treatment strategy.

The antecedents of a particular behavior are the times, people, places, or things that consistently appear in the patient's environment just before the behavior occurs. In the past these stimuli have been repeatedly associated with the behavior, although they need not have had a direct causal effect. The repeated presence of these stimuli prior to the behavior's occurrence has been sufficient for the behavior to have become associated with them and eventually to be elicited by them. For example, an obese patient may observe that, whereas in the past he regularly felt hungry at noon and ate lunch, currently he begins to prepare his lunch at noon each day, regardless of the degree of hunger he is experiencing. Changing his eating habits so that he eats in response to feelings of hunger rather than to the hour of day might be an important goal for this patient.

Similarly, an acrophobic patient (one who is afraid of heights) may feel considerable anxiety when he looks at a tall building, although he remains standing on the street below. A treatment goal for this patient might be to reduce the anxiety he feels when looking up at skyscrapers. For these two patients the stimuli of time and tall buildings act as cues that trigger the problem behaviors of eating and fear, respectively.

The consequences of the problem-behavior pattern are of equal importance. The behaviorist views a person's actions as operating on the environment to produce a specific result: a pleasant event, such as love, food, or attention (positive reinforcement), or an unpleasant event such as pain, anxiety, or nausea (punishment). On the other hand, the behavior may result in the withdrawal of a pleasant event (also punishment) or the withdrawal of an unpleasant event (negative reinforcement). The nature of the consequences following a person's actions influences the probability that he will perform the same behavior in similar situations in the future.

In addition to identifying the nature of the consequences following a problem behavior, the behavior therapist also evaluates systematically the pattern of these consequences. While a particular behavior of a patient may result in a specific consequence each time it occurs, more commonly a consequence occurs only after the behavior has appeared several times, or some time has elapsed after its performance. Since the frequency with which a consequence follows a particular behavior has considerable influence on the behavior, the therapist examines this relation carefully.

Clinicians have found that behaviors that have been irregularly followed by immediate positive consequences tend to be among the most enduring behaviors. While undesirable behaviors having this pattern of reinforcement are the most difficult for the patient to change, it is also this reinforcement pattern that the clinician attempts to establish for the patient's new appropriate behaviors. For example, a treatment goal for an agoraphobic patient (one fearful of leaving the house) would be to increase the frequency and duration of the patient's trips away from home. In treating this patient the therapist would carefully attend to the pattern of positive reinforcement experienced by the patient during each trip. Initially, immediate and frequent social support for the patient's attempts to walk greater distances from the house would be planned. Gradually, however, the frequency at which the therapist offered reinforcement would be reduced until eventually the intermittent, natural, pleasant consequences of visiting public places and participating in community activities would be sufficient to support the patient's new behavior.

Returning to the case of Mr. G., the following functional analysis was made:

> After specifying that Mr. G.'s problem behaviors were a combination of anxious feelings and thoughts experienced in social situations, the therapist attempted to identify their antecedents and consequences.
>
> The patient's log revealed several consistent antecedents for his behaviors. While Mr. G. experienced these thoughts and feelings

in any social situation, they were stronger if he did not know the person, milder if the person was a casual acquaintance, and absent if he knew the person well. This was the case with associates at work and his neighbors at home.

The consequences of Mr. G.'s anxieties were manifold. When the self-critical thoughts arose, he tried to show the other person how intelligent he was. He would "play one-up-manship." Unfortunately, the other person often took offense and occasionally an argument would ensue. Once this type of interaction began, Mr. G. felt that he was compelled to win the argument in order to maintain his self-esteem.

The functional analysis of this situation was that Mr. G.'s concerns about how another person was perceiving him produced an intolerable anxiety for him. As a result, he would attempt to reduce this anxiety by demonstrating his intelligence and competence. These attempts consistently resulted in an immediate decrease in his anxiety. This decrease in anxiety increased the likelihood that he would behave similarly in future encounters to reduce his anxiety. Typically, however, the other person would lose interest in talking with him again. On the other hand, when Mr. G. tried to resist playing one-up-manship, he became increasingly anxious, since he believed that the other person interpreted his silence as an indication that he "had nothing to say and was therefore not very intelligent."

During the therapy sessions Mr. G. showed that he could in fact discuss a wide variety of topics with ease and had considerable interpersonal skill. It was apparent that while he could perform the appropriate interpersonal behaviors quite well when he was relaxed, his anxieties and self-critical thoughts occurred in stressful or unfamiliar situations. Although Mr. G. was aware of this pattern, he could not change his behavior. The task of therapy was therefore to elicit his appropriate social skills and relaxed feelings in these problem situations.

BEHAVIORAL TREATMENT

Strongly influenced by the methods of experimental psychology, the behavior therapist proceeds in designing a treatment strategy with the awareness that he must be able to identify objectively the effects of therapy on the patient's problem behavior. These effects must be evaluated on the basis of information that could be observed or measured by other mental health professionals. Unless it can be shown that the intervention strategy has altered the patient's functioning in a demonstrable manner, then there is little support for a claim of having implemented an effective treatment.

While the behaviorist views the therapist's own feelings as valuable aids in the design of the patient's treatment, they are not considered sufficient for concluding that the treatment was successful. Throughout therapy, therefore, the behavior therapist attempts to obtain objective observations of the problem-behavior patterns. This data is used to gauge the patient's progress and adjust the treatment strategy when necessary. If, for example, the behavior therapist believes that a patient's phobic anxiety has diminished, this must be demonstrated by objective measurements in addition to the patient's subjective feelings or the therapist's intuitive judgment. For this purpose, the therapist may have the patient enter the feared situation while recording anxiety-related physical responses such as trembling, sweating, heart rate, or distance from the feared object.

Behavior therapists have gradually accumulated descriptions of cause-effect relations that consistently influence patients' behavior in specific ways. In addition, a variety of instruments have been designed for use in assessing behavior change. While relying heavily on social learning theory for direction, behavior therapists will embrace a therapeutic procedure regardless of the theoretical "school" from which the practice arises if changes in a patient's functioning following such treatment can be demonstrated. In a real sense, behavior therapists attempt to combine the experimental eye of the research psychologist with the intuitive clinical skills of the psychotherapist.

Some of the strategies commonly used in behavior therapy are positive control, systematic desensitization, aversive control, extinction, and modeling. These methods can be applied individually and in combination to a variety of behavior patterns in adults and children.

Positive control

One of the strategies most widely used to modify problem behavior has been the systematic presentation of *positive reinforcement* to the patient upon his completion of a desired behavior. Since the occurrence of a behavior is directly influenced by its consequences, reinforcement that follows the behavior immediately will increase the probability that the behavior will be repeated under similar conditions in the future (Skinner, 1953).

The importance of the therapist's positive reinforcement of the patient's behavior is easily seen in the effects of the therapist's attention on the patient's verbal behavior. The content of a patient's conversation is directly influenced not only by the therapist's reinforcing statements (e.g., "yes," "tell me more," or "you handled that nicely"), but also by his non-verbal actions (e.g., head nodding, eye contact, or leaning forward in chair). It has been demonstrated that the extent to which the patient's speech contains emotional expressions, statements of personal beliefs, early childhood memories, "neurotic" references, and favorable or unfavorable self-statements can be directly influenced by reinforcement from the therapist (Kanfer, 1968; Krasner, 1962).

A more explicit application of positive reinforcement occurs in the use of a contract between patient and therapist. In a contract the therapist and patient identify a specific situation in which the patient is to perform a particular behavior at a given time. The contract also includes the reinforcement which the patient will obtain when the contract is fulfilled and the aversive consequences that will occur if he fails to do so. For example, a therapist might establish a contract with a depressed patient that would require the patient to participate each day for one week in at least one social activity which had been reinforcing to the patient before his current depression. If the patient complied with the contract, then the therapist would agree to discuss in therapy any topic of the patient's choice. If, however, the patient failed to fulfill the contract, the patient agreed to review with the therapist the problems the patient had experienced with the contract. Of course, in this contract it is assumed that talking to the therapist about "any topic of the patient's choice" is a reinforcing activity for the patient and that participating in social activities, while a desirable treatment goal, is a difficult if not unpleasant activity for the patient. In subsequent therapy sessions, however, the therapist and patient would renegotiate the contract to include other positive or negative consequences for additional behaviors.

Contracts have proven to be an effective tool in a wide variety of inpatient and outpatient therapeutic settings where changes in a patient's behavior are indicated and the patient lacks the self-management skills to implement them. Moreover, contracts have been particularly successful when used with adults and children in schools, clinics, and institutional settings.

Reinforcement principles have also been used in the design of *token systems*. Like a contract, a token system explicitly states the reinforcement which an individual can obtain. The unique feature of this method, however, is that tokens rather than an actual reinforcement item are earned for the performance of a particular behavior. These tokens may be in the form of chips, stars, points, or other markers. The tokens are then exchanged at a future time for the desired reinforcement (e.g., privileges, special events, or material items). A token system enables staff members responsible for a large group of people to reinforce promptly the desired behavior of an individual without interrupting an ongoing activity. Punishment in the form of fines can also be administered quickly for undesired behaviors. Token systems have been successfully used in schools, inpatient psychiatric wards, special education programs, adolescent treatment facilities, and rehabilitation programs (Ayllon and Azrin, 1968; Kanfer and Phillips, 1970).

Systematic desensitization

In 1958 Joseph Wolpe described what is now a standard behavioral approach to the treatment of inappropriate fears and anxieties: *systematic desensitization*. This procedure is frequently used with patients who realize that their anxiety is irrational (i.e., fear of crowded places, medications, being alone, or heights) but still are unable to remain relaxed and comfortable in the feared situation. The procedure is based on the observation that usually a person will experience only the stronger of two competing emotional responses. For example, a patient will report feelings of anxiety or of relaxation, but not both at the same time. Therefore, Wolpe reasoned, neurotic anxieties could be reduced if a state of deep muscle relaxation could be induced and maintained while the patient imagined mild anxiety-producing situations related to the phobia. When the patient's fear subsided in response to these mild anxiety-producing situations, he would imagine progressively more fearful situations. Even images that had been very frightening would eventually lose their ability to produce anxiety.

Current systematic desensitization procedures usually involve three separate steps: 1. training the patient in deep muscle relaxation; 2. constructing with the patient a hierarchy of scenes involving the feared situation, from least feared to most feared; and 3. systematically directing the patient to imagine each fearful scene in the hierarchy while remaining deeply relaxed.

For example, if a patient has a fear of heights so intense that he can not ascend a building past the second floor, the therapist might initially teach the patient how to reduce the tension he felt in each part of his body and maintain a deeply relaxed state. The patient would be trained to differentiate the sensation of tension produced when his muscles are flexed from the sensation of relaxation when they are relaxed. The patient would gradually learn to detect even the slightest muscle tension and effectively eliminate it.

Once this skill was mastered, the therapist would help the patient construct a hierarchy of images to his fear, from most fearful (i.e., standing on the twelfth floor of a building and looking down at the ground) to the least fearful (i.e., walking past a twelve-story building. Finally, the patient would be instructed to imagine each step in the hierarchy from least fearful to most fearful while remaining deeply relaxed. The goal of systematic desensitization is not only to enable the patient to imagine himself in the feared situations without feeling anxiety, but also to experience *actually* the previously feared situation without experiencing anxiety. Further desensitizations together with practice in the actual situation is later used as often as needed for situations that continue to produce anxiety.

Aversive control

Aversive techniques are used in behavior therapy to eliminate behavior patterns considered harmful to the patient or to those around him. In these situations a painful event is arranged to occur immediately after the undesirable behavior. Through consistent association of the aversive event with the behavior, the patient learns to refrain from performing the behavior in similar situations in the future. Aversive consequences such as painful electric shock and nausea-inducing drugs have been used with patients engaging in a variety of inappropriate or addictive behaviors including sexual deviance, exhibitionism, smoking, head banging, drug addiction, and alcoholism.

Aversive techniques are rarely used in isolation, however. Since the therapist's goal is not simply to remove an inappropriate behavior pattern but to establish and maintain permanent appropriate behavior, aversive techniques are used in combination with other procedures that will teach the desired behavior once it occurs. Hence, whenever aversive techniques are implemented, a reinforcement system for the desired behavior is usually also part of the therapy.

For example, the drug disulfiram (Antabuse) will produce nausea, copious vomiting, and vertigo if a patient who has taken it drinks even a small amount of alcohol. Behavior therapists have used this effect in carefully supervised programs to create an aversion toward any alcoholic beverage in alcoholic patients who wish to stop drinking. In addition to this aversive treatment, however, the patients also participate in programs designed to promote and support appropriate non-alcohol-related behavior. Thus, a patient might receive positive social reinforcement for performing the desired behavior of refusing a drink in various simulated situations.

Extreme caution must be exercised in applying any aversive technique. The use of punishment raises serious ethical issues and also has the potential for creating unwanted side effects. Aversive techniques may teach the patient to fear the person administering the punishment (i.e., the punished child may become afraid of the punisher). Equally undesirable, the person administering the punishment may be acting inadvertently as a model for behavior as undesirable as that being punished (i.e., the punished child may attempt to control other children's behavior with punishment). Further, the use of punishment requires careful planning for a proper generalization of its effects so as to avoid the result of eliminating the undesirable behavior only in the specific situations where the threat of punishment exists (i.e., the punished child refrains from performing the undesired behavior only when an adult is present).

Extinction

When the positive consequences that had previously followed a behavior are withheld, the behavior occurs less and less frequently until eventually it is extinguished. Ayllon and Haughton (1964) used extinction procedures with two chronic schizophrenic women who voiced continual complaints of medical problems in the absence of any physical disease or illness. When the staff of the psychiatric unit withdrew its attention from the women if they complained, the number of complaints dropped from approximately 170 per day to near 0.

The extinction principle is used also in implosive therapy (Stampfl and Lewis, 1967), which involves continually exposing a phobic patient to a highly feared object, animal, or situation. Implosive therapy is based on the phobic person's fear that a catastrophic event will occur if he performs a particular behavior. If, however, he repeatedly performs the feared behavior, and the imagined disaster does not happen, his anxiety should decrease.

To illustrate this technique, Stampfl and Lewis described a patient who was terrified of dirt and continually washed his hands. The therapists used implosive therapy by instructing the patient to repeatedly imagine himself covered with filth. As the patient repeatedly did so, his fear of dirt was slowly extinguished, and the frequency of his hand-washing diminished.

Bandura (1969) has suggested that the extinction process may in fact be an important aspect of all forms of psychotherapy. Viewing the typical therapeutic relation as permissive and supportive, he notes that the patient in therapy is encouraged to express thoughts and feelings that were previously punished or had aroused extreme anxiety and guilt. The therapist's acceptance of the patient's expression of these feelings or thoughts eventually reduces the emotional reactions associated with them. Bandura hypothesizes that abreaction procedures in which patients experience past traumatic events while under hypnosis or the influence of drugs may have similar effects in extinguishing fear or anxiety responses.

Modeling

Modeling is also a potentially powerful method for initiating new behavior or eliminating undesirable behavior. In this procedure the patient is presented with a model who demonstrates the behavior to be acquired. The patient learns how the model acts in a given situation and, more importantly, vicariously experiences the positive or aversive results of the modeled behavior. The patient is then encouraged to imitate the model's behavior in a simulated situation and eventually to perform the new behavior instead of the inappropriate behavior in the problem situation.

Modeling has been used to reduce fears and teach adults and children a variety of behaviors including assertive actions, sexual behavior, social conduct, and decision-making skills. Lovaas and his colleagues (1967) used the technique of modeling to teach autistic children to imitate speech. These children were not only mute but often engaged in repetitive self-stimulatory behavior (i.e., staring at an object, rocking, grimacing). Combining modeling with reinforcement and punishment techniques, the clinicians initially taught these children to observe carefully and imitate accurately a model's words and behavior. Soon the children learned to repeat entire sentences and follow verbal instructions. Gradually they learned to describe events and objects around them with their newly acquired speech.

Modeling has been applied also when the behavior to be taught must be performed *in toto* in the environment in order for the patient to receive reinforcement or avoid punishment. It is a particularly useful technique in situations where it is not possible or desirable for the patient to acquire the behavior gradually. For example, a patient who lacks specific interpersonal skills (i.e., is inappropriately aggressive) could observe a model who demonstrates appropriate behaviors in social situations (i.e., listens to others, accepts others' opinions, and refrains from using abusive language). The patient would be instructed to imitate the modeled behavior in an actual social situation. In this way, the patient is given the opportunity to receive social reinforcement in the natural environment for a combination of appropriate social behaviors which, if learned one at a time, would not have been supported (i.e., if the patient learned to accept others' opinions but continued to use abusive language, the patient's difficulties would persist).

Covert behavior

While behavior therapists have traditionally focused on a patient's overt or visible behavior, behavioral methods have recently been applied to patients' thoughts and images, their covert behavior (Homme, 1965). If a patient is experiencing thoughts that are self-critical, illogical, or repetitive, then one of the aims of the therapeutic program is to assist him in modifying these covert behaviors.

Covert behavioral approaches assume that a patient's thoughts and images are governed by the same learning principles that influence his observable behavior. The behavior therapist, therefore, uses treatment methods similar in principle to those applied to overt behavior. Each treatment strategy discussed in this chapter has, with some modification, been applied to covert behavior. For example, Horan and Johnson (1971) have used covert positive thoughts (i.e., "My clothes will fit properly") as reinforcing consequences for an obese patient who resisted the urge to eat. Cautela (1966) used covert aversive thoughts (i.e., the image of oneself vomiting) as a punishing consequence for the impulse to smoke. With covert modeling, Meichenbaum and Cameron (1974) have taught patients to change their self-talk and, as a result, modify their overt behavior. They encouraged schizophrenic patients to follow self-instructions and to "give healthy talk, be coherent and relevant" in order to reduce the amount of "crazy talk" in an interview setting. Similarly, phobic patients have been taught to reduce their anxiety when engaged in a previously feared activity, by instructing themselves to remain relaxed, take one step at a time, and maintain their determination to master the situation.

As with all behavior therapy, attempts to modify covert behavior must clearly specify which behavior is the target of treatment. In addition, the therapist must carefully design observation methods for the patient to record the incidence of each covert behavior, so that the effects of treatment can be determined. Programs combining covert and overt treatment strategies offer behavior therapists increasingly effective methods for helping patients to initiate and maintain permanent behavior change.

The therapeutic program

Behavior therapists typically combine several treatment strategies in the design of an overall therapeutic program for each patient. For example, a therapist working with a depressed patient may use *modeling* to demonstrate appropriate assertive behaviors, *contracting* to encourage him to increase the number of enjoyable activities engaged in each day, *positive reinforcement* to support his initiation of social interaction, *extinction* by withholding attention to decrease his repeated reference to past unpleasant events, and *covert self-instruction* to interrupt his depressing thoughts. Each strategy within the therapeutic program is aimed at a particular aspect of the patient's problem behavior.

Implicit in any behavioral program is the therapist's goal of withdrawing the treatment strategies as soon as possible. The program should be designed so that the patient's new behavior will generalize to the natural environment and will eventually be supported by natural positive consequences. To make this possible, the therapist selects situations that increasingly simulate each real situation in which the patient must perform the appropriate behavior. The therapist also gradually reduces the patient's dependence on the treatment strategies and slowly withdraws his reinforcement of the patient's new behavior. Behavior therapists recognize that the true goal of therapy is not merely to change a patient's behavior while he is in treatment, but also to give him self-management skills so that the behavioral changes initiated in therapy will endure.

The case of Mr. G. can be introduced again to illustrate a behavior therapy program and the eventual maintenance of the patient's new behavior by his social environment:

> The therapist designed a modified systematic desensitization program for Mr. G. Initially he was taught a deep muscle relaxation procedure and instructed to practice it daily at home. Once Mr. G. could readily achieve a relaxed state, a hierarchy of anxiety-producing social situations was created. Mr. G. then imagined each of these scenes while maintaining a deeply relaxed state. When he was relaxed, Mr. G. also repeated to himself one of three highly positive thoughts which he strongly believed to be true about himself.
>
> Once Mr. G. could remain relaxed while imagining each scene in the hierarchy, a contract was written between the therapist and the patient in which Mr. G. was to seek a particular social situation each day to practice maintaining his relaxed feelings and positive thoughts about himself. After each encounter Mr. G. recorded in a log book his anxiety and the number of self-critical thoughts he experienced in the situation.

The therapist reviewed the log book with Mr. G. and offered support and positive reinforcement for Mr. G.'s successful mastery of each difficult social interaction. In addition he examined with Mr. G. those situations in which he continued to be anxious. As the number of anxious and self-critical thoughts in social situations decreased, Mr. G. began to enjoy being with people more frequently and reported that he was receiving more invitations to join other people in group activities. As Mr. G. experienced increasing success, his social environment began to support this new behavior. Gradually the contract with the therapist was discontinued, and fewer therapy sessions were scheduled.

Six months later Mr. G.'s log reflected that he was feeling anxious about once a week in social situations, and he rarely needed to use the relaxation or positive-thought techniques. According to his own statement, he now felt comfortable in social situations and had acquired a very positive view of himself.

REFERENCES

American Psychiatric Association Task Force Report, *Behavior Therapy in Psychiatry*. Washington, D.C.: APA, 1974.

Ayllon, T., and Azrin, N. *The Token Economy: A Motivational System for Therapy and Rehabilitation*. New York: Appleton-Century-Crofts, 1968.

Ayllon, T., and Haughton, E. "Modifications of Symptomatic Verbal Behavior of Mental Patients." *Behavior Research and Therapy* 2:87–94, 1964.

Bandura, A. *Principles of Behavior Modification*. New York: Holt, Rinehart and Winston, 1969.

Cautela, J. R. "Covert Conditioning." In *The Psychology of Private Events: Perspective on Covert Response Systems*, ed. by A. Jacobs and L. B. Sachs. New York: Academic Press, 1971, pp. 190–230.

Homme, L. E. "Perspectives in Psychology, XXIV: Control of coverants, the operants of the mind." *Psychological Record* 15: 501–11, 1965.

Horan, J. J., and Johnson, R. G. "Coverant Conditioning through Self-management Application of the Premack Principle: Its effects on weight reduction." *Journal of Behavior Therapy and Experimental Psychiatry* 2:243–49, 1971.

Kanfer, F. H. "Verbal conditioning: A review of its current states." In

Verbal Behavior and General Behavior Theory, ed. by T. R. Dixon and D. C. Horton. Englewood Cliffs, N.J.: Prentice Hall, pp. 254–90, 1968.

Kanfer, F. H., and Phillips, J. *Learning Foundations of Behavior Therapy*, New York: Wiley, 1970.

Krasner, L. "The psychotherapist as a social reinforced machine." In *Research in Psychotherapy* II, ed. by H. H. Strup and L. Luborsky. Washington, D.C.: American Psychological Association, pp. 61–94, 1962.

Lovaas, O. I. "A behavior therapy approach to the treatment of childhood schizophrenia." In *Minnesota Symposia on Child Psychology* I, ed. by O. P. Hill. Minneapolis: University of Minnesota Press, pp. 108–59, 1967.

Meichenbaum, D. H., and Cameron, R. "The Clinical Potential and Pitfalls of Modifying What Clients Say to Themselves." In *Self-Control: Power to the Person*, ed. by M. J. Mahoney and C. E. Thorsen. Monterey, Calif.: Brooks College, 1974.

Skinner, B. F. *Science and Human Behavior*. New York: Free Press, 1953.

Stampfl, T. G., and Lewis, D. J. "Essentials of Implosive Therapy: A learning based psychodynamic behavioral therapy." *Journal of Abnormal Psychology*, 72:496–503, 1967.

10

GROUP PSYCHOTHERAPY

Troubled persons were meeting in groups to deal with their emotional distress long before psychotherapy as such evolved. The practice has been used to reduce tensions between members of organized groups, as well as to help individual members cope with their personal problems. An interesting example, described by Johnson (1963), is the Chapter of Faults tradition that has existed among Benedictine monks for some fourteen hundred years—and all later monastic foundations. This is a regularly scheduled meeting, one or more times a week, at which the monks criticize themselves and each other as they strive for self-perfection. This meeting is conducted by the superior of the house and is characterized by confessions, confrontations, admonitions, advice, encouragement, and support.

The practice of group psychotherapy on the part of health professionals has become increasingly widespread since its beginnings early in the twentieth century. In recent years it has become one of the fastest growing subspecialties in psychiatry.

Sadock (1975) defines group psychotherapy as a form of treatment in which carefully selected emotionally-ill persons are placed in a group so that, under the guidance of a trained therapist, they can help each other effect personality change. Many therapists would view this definition as too narrow; more broadly, it is a form of psychotherapy in which the therapist's efforts to enhance patients' feelings of well-being, reduce their psychological discomfort, or improve their social functioning are conducted with a group of patients. These aims can be undertaken through the use of any of the approaches described in preceding chapters, such as insight, support, or behavioral methods. What Levine has said of psychotherapy in general—that it provides new life experiences—applies equally to group therapy.

Group psychotherapy was apparently introduced into medicine by Joseph Pratt, a Boston internist, in 1905. Dr. Pratt organized a group of tuberculosis patients to instuct them in methods of physical hygiene. But the typical emotional problems of tuberculosis patients in that era—discouragement, lowered self-esteem, rejection by others—gave the group meetings an unexpected function of providing support and reassurance through discussion of shared experiences.

Alfred Adler, at one time a follower of Freud, evolved his own variation of analytic therapy, stressing the development of social interests and constructive cooperation with others. He was one of the first psychotherapists to advocate and use group meetings to achieve therapeutic goals. Ernst Simmel, another early psychoanalyst, used group psychotherapy in the German Army during World War I to treat psychiatric casualties. Didactic approaches to group psychotherapy were expounded by Lazell (1919) and L. Cody Marsh (1935), who both used lectures and a classroom format in group sessions. Marsh even graded his subjects on their comprehension of the material presented and on a wide range of behavior including punctuality, cooperation, and judgment. This didactic approach is now rarely practiced (Enelow and Wexler, 1966).

World War II gave great impetus to group therapy. For the military services it was an economical way to provide psychotherapy to large numbers of military personnel. Many psychiatrists and psychologists who learned to use group therapy in military service introduced it into their clinical practice after the war. Although before World War II some therapists had been practicing insight-oriented group therapy and psychodrama, it was now given much wider application toward more varied goals.

GROUP PROCESS

"Group process" is the term often applied by therapists to the patterns of interaction that emerge during group psychotherapy. Sometimes it is used also to describe the characteristics that those writing on the topic believe to be held in common by group therapies regardless of the objectives or style of therapy. "Group dynamics" is a commonly used synonym for "group process." Some of these authors believe that groups have stages or phases of development. Schutz (1958), for example, described the course of group therapy in three stages: *inclusion*, or the period in which patients are concerned about being loved or accepted, and belonging; *power*, or the period in which patients seek autonomy from the leader and challenge his power; and *affection*, in which patients are concerned with equality and with giving affection as well as taking it. Others define group process in a way to suggest that there need be no predictable pattern but that certain themes tend to appear in all group therapy.

Each group is of course unique. Some are warm and friendly; others are tense with conflict; still others tend to break into cliques. But some events are common to all groups. For example, early in the history of each group, the therapist is seen as a group leader (whether that is his intent), the most important member of the group. Patients look to the leader for guidance and try to behave in ways they perceive to be what he wants. In successful group therapy, a sense of cohesion begins to develop in the group before long. Group members begin to feel committed to each other and to the common undertaking. Strong feelings emerge toward both the therapist and fellow patients. Often one or more members of the group will attempt to assert a leadership role, perhaps in competition with the therapist or perhaps as his unofficial auxiliary. Conflicts between group members are likely to become sharper as roles take shape within the group. These reflect each person's characteristic ways of responding to others, and such responses then become the focus of the group's discussions. There will be different responses to group pressures; and how they are handled by the therapist will, of course, vary with the type of therapy practiced. Certain members may try to dominate, to remain passive, to be autonomous yet still within the group, or to withdraw from participation. Whatever his approach, the therapist will have to observe closely these interpersonal configurations.

Some "open-ended" therapy groups allow members to join or leave the group at any point. The patterns of interaction in such groups are altered whenever a new member enters or an old member leaves. Also, the leader tends to remain an important focus of the group's feelings in these less stable groups. If the group has developed a strong sense of cohesiveness, a new member may find himself struggling to become a part of the group. Some groups are open in nature, welcoming new members and striving to give them a sense of belonging. Others tend to be exclusive, resisting the inclusion of new members. Similarly, new members may strive for inclusion or resist it. An important part of the therapist's job is to respond to these events and the feelings surrounding them in ways that will facilitate the group's effort to reach its goals.

Some groups are time-limited, some go on indefinitely, and some (by virtue of being open-ended) are constantly, though gradually, changing, as old members leave and new members enter. In each case the group process is significantly influenced by the leadership or therapeutic style of the group therapist. Some therapists emphasize the authority inherent in the role of therapist, and "conduct" the therapy. Such therapists tend to focus on problems occurring outside the group; and though there may be some discussion of the group's response to its strong leader, this type of therapy tends to be more didactic than other approaches. Other therapists diminish the sense of difference between their status as professionals and the members' status as patients by allowing the group a great deal of freedom in determining the form and content of the discussion, and refraining from indicating which direction it should take. Therapists who focus on the interactions that take place during the sessions—the immediate group process—are most likely to bring to the surface conflicts between group members, between individual members and the therapist, and between the group as a whole and the therapist. Therapists who give more attention to accounts of events that have occurred outside the therapy session engage the group in more analysis of the behavior of individual members.

Insight-oriented group therapy

This is sometimes referred to as "analytic" group therapy. As in one-to-one insight-oriented therapy, the main goal is to understand one's own behavior. The group process, however, inevitably fosters an emphasis on understanding one's own behavior in relation to others. Patients are selected for such therapy largely on the basis of their interest in, and capacity for, self-understanding. They are usually suffering neurosis or minor personality disorders, or are dissatisfied with their social adjustment and desirous of changing their behavior. Therapists who use this approach usually try to facilitate free, unstructured communication, especially at the beginning, allowing patients who wish to speak about something to take the lead.

Interpretations tend to center on past events considered to be determinants of a member's behavior toward others in the group or of the behavior patterns that characterize his everyday life. The group interaction serves primarily as a setting to evoke the members' individual psychological problems or to highlight their social difficulties. When a patient talks about problems that occur outside the group, the therapist may or may not relate them to the person's behavior in the group. When he does not, the parallel with individual insight therapy is closer. When he does, the therapy takes on a more process-oriented flavor.

Although all insight therapies aim for self-understanding, there are differences depending on the "school" to which the therapist belongs. A psychoanalyst conducting group therapy tends to address himself to transference and resistance, and to view the interactions between each person and others in the group as reflective of relationships formed in childhood. Adlerians, on the other hand, try to give the patient more understanding of his social functioning, particularly his ability to cooperate with others as reflected in the group interaction. Though they pay less attention to the past than psychoanalysts, the Adlerians do explore the historical roots of such behavior. As in all therapy, the therapist's conceptual model strongly influences the kinds of behavior he focuses on and the kinds of interpretations he makes.

Kaplan and Sadock (1971) have described a variant of analytic group therapy which they call "structured interactional group psychotherapy." In contrast to most analytic group therapy, this approach requires the therapist to take specific steps to ensure the participation of each patient. At each session the group discussion centers on a particular member previously selected by the therapist. This patient is expected to talk about himself for fifteen or twenty minutes. The group as a whole then discusses this patient's statements, expressions of feeling, and behavior. In this general discussion each member of the group is encouraged to reveal his response to the patient who opened the session. In addition, the therapist may introduce other techniques borrowed from other approaches to therapy. These include some behavior modification procedures, some psychodrama, and the use of audio-tape recordings.

Process-oriented group therapy

In process-oriented group therapy, as in individual process-oriented therapy, the therapist encourages free, unstructured communication and pays attention to the way in which patients communicate with him and with other group members. His comments are directed to the patient's behavior in the same here-and-now manner described in Chapter 5. The therapist is concerned with what is going on during the therapy session itself, rather than with outside events in the recent or more remote past. He may comment on the tone of voice or non-verbal communication manifested in the patient's behavior toward him or the other group members. Inconsistencies between content and process in the patient's communication, and any artificiality or indirectness, are likely to evoke his comment. The group members will usually begin to respond to each other, as well as to the therapist, in a similar fashion. Thus, the therapist's behavior sometimes becomes the subject of observations made by the patients. In this type of group therapy (which is modeled on Kaiser's individual therapy) the difference in status between therapist and patient is less clear than in many other types.

Transactional analysis
In almost all group psychotherapy, of course, more attention is paid to the process than to the content of the patients' communication, though some group therapists work as though they were performing individual psychotherapy in the presence of the group. A middle ground between process- and insight-oriented group therapy is "transactional analysis" (see Chapter 5). Transactional analysts use the Parent, Adult, and Child model to describe different "ego states" or styles of communicating with and relating to others, and they interpret interpersonal behavior in terms of "transactions." They pay close attention to the group process but place it within this theoretical framework. Thus, the patient is told about his rituals, his games, and his pastimes—usually those involving other members of the group, though not excluding those described in their other relations.

Eric Berne (1966), founder of transactional analysis, saw the therapist's behavior as having four main functions: to interpret the particular ego state of that moment for the patient—i.e., parent, adult, or child; to encourage the patient to utilize an adult ego state; to help the patient understand what he is doing and which parts of his personality are involved in the "game," and thus give him more control over whether he continues to play it; to help the patient "change his script." Transactional analysis is usually conducted as group therapy but often resembles individual therapy carried out in a group setting.

"Rogerian" therapy

Group therapists who espouse the concepts of Carl Rogers aim for the expression of feelings experienced by group members toward one another during sessions, whether the feelings are positive or negative. This is achieved only gradually. First, the resistance to such expression is discussed. Then group members talk about feelings experienced in the past, and finally, in a successful group, the patients express feelings as they are experienced.

The therapist's activity consists largely of clarifying what he thinks members are trying to express. As therapy proceeds, members tend to do so for each other. This is believed to lead gradually to acceptance of one's feelings and finally to self-acceptance, the goal of Rogerian therapy. In this type of therapy, a greater degree of freedom to feel and express positive feelings would likely be a successful outcome.

Group behavior therapy

The principles of behavior therapy described in Chapter 9 can be applied in a group setting, and often are more effective when this is done. Like process-oriented therapy, behavior therapy concentrates on the here-and-now, particularly the interactions during therapeutic sessions. The group may have a single therapeutic objective—such as changing eating behavior in an effort to lose weight, or the patients may share a variety of similar goals. The behavioral techniques most often used in group therapy are *feedback, modeling, behavior rehearsal, desensitization, assertiveness training,* and *social reinforcement* (Goldstein and Wolpe, 1971).

Feedback is accomplished when members are encouraged to respond as honestly and openly as possible toward one another, which should make each person more aware of the connections between one's behavior and the responses of others. The aim is to help each patient learn to distinguish whatever behavior of his elicits undesirable responses from behavior that elicits desirable responses.

Modeling is a matter of observing others in the group performing the behavior that is to be learned. The best model is usually the therapist himself. Modeling may occur spontaneously or it may be deliberately employed. One technique for introducing modeling into therapy is role-playing, which can be done between patients or with the therapist.

In a *behavior rehearsal* a patient with a specific problem role-plays a new type of behavior, one that he can use in real life situations on encountering that problem. Feedback is given, and so is reinforcement for effective performances.

Desensitization is a procedure designed to reduce gradually or eliminate the capacity of a given stimulus to elicit anxiety, fear, or guilt from a person. Usually this involves actual exposure of the person to the stimulus in graded doses beginning with a very small one. Desensitization can be facilitated in groups when the fear centers on activities involving groups.

Wolpe (1973) reports a desensitization of eight subjects, all of whom were participants in a seminar on behavior therapy. The procedure was carried out in front of the class of thirty students. At the beginning of the course, participants who feared public speaking were invited to volunteer for desensitization. Each treatment session took place at the end of a two-hour seminar. Five of the eight subjects went through the entire period and were helped in five treatment sessions—a very brief course of therapy. As this indicates, specific behavior therapy procedures for a single symptom tend to be completed within a relatively brief period.

Assertiveness training is still another type of behavior therapy that is used with groups. It consists of role-playing appropriately assertive responses by patients who have been overly compliant or timid and who have felt anxious when tempted to express feelings, whether negative (e.g., annoyance complaints, differences of opinion) or positive (e.g., affection, admiration, praise). Reinforcement is given for the assertive behavior in the group.

Social reinforcement and group pressure are, of course, powerful motivating factors in changing attitudes and behavior and in ensuring that the changes last.

Group behavior therapy is being used more widely now in efforts to alter health-related behavior such as over-eating, smoking, and no-exercise habits.

PSYCHODRAMA

Psychodrama is psychotherapy "on stage." It is almost always carried out with groups of patients. Psychodrama was conceived and developed by J. L. Moreno, who had been doing group psychotherapy as early as 1914, and by 1922 had created a theater setting in Vienna where people could gather and take part in improvised, scriptless plays. From this "theater of spontaneity," as Moreno called it, came many of the ideas that led to role-playing in psychotherapy, role-training methods, and psychodrama. Moreno's description of his method (1971) is the basis for the following summary.

Psychodrama sessions usually focus on a problem or problem situation of one patient—the "actor." The therapist is referred to as the "director." The other patients in the group, called "auxiliary egos," are assigned specific roles by the director. Some of these roles are unique to psychodrama and will be described below. Moreno prefers to use a special psychodrama stage, but any room with sufficient space will do.

The patient who is to be the actor for a given session chooses the conflict, problem, fantasy, or troublesome relationship that he wishes to act out. He provides enough information so that the "supporting cast" needed can be chosen by the director. As the session proceeds, however, all members will have a part in the action. Rather than talking about the past, the actor-patient recreates the situation "on stage." He is encouraged to be spontaneous, but not necessarily accurate, in portraying the situation. Fact and memory can be mixed with fantasy, or the actor may choose to portray a pure fantasy or daydream. He is also encouraged by the director to exaggerate his expressions and actions, even to distort or misrepresent his feelings. In Moreno's view, genuine restraint and objectivity, as differentiated from neurotic inhibition, can be attained only after the most subjective and unrestrained expression of feelings has been experienced.

At the outset the therapist tries to deal with relatively minor problems rather than the actor-patient's deepest concerns. But the patient may take over the direction of the scene, rejecting or altering the therapist's directions. He may, even, if he wishes, assume the role of director for his own psychodrama. In that event the patient picks the scene and whatever "auxiliary egos" he needs to produce his psychodrama. Such "auxiliary egos" may take the roles of other characters in the psychodrama, or they may be "doubles"— in which case the auxiliary ego represents the patient. The double may move in concert with the actor-patient, and may echo his words and behave like him, but he may add his own elaboration of the thoughts and feelings expressed by the patient. The actor and the auxiliary ego may discuss the actor's feelings as though they were two aspects of the same person. The actor-patient may choose to have several doubles, or the director-therapist may assign them to him. Then each auxiliary ego portrays what is considered to be a facet of the actor's personality, as when his feelings are mixed or his attitudes have changed from the past to the present.

Role reversal may be called for by the director or the patient if either believes that this will increase the actor's understanding of how others view him or respond to him. In this case the patient who is portraying a scene with another person may exchange roles with that person.

The patient may also choose, or be instructed by the director, to present a soliloquy. This is a verbal presentation by the patient of such thoughts or feelings of his as are considered too complex to be adequately portrayed by action. The soliloquy is followed by a psychodrama designed to resolve what has been expressed or to relate it to earlier parts of the session.

Psychodrama is not bound to any single conceptual model of personality development or of neurosis. If interpretations are offered, they will reflect the therapist's orientation. Behavior therapists have used psychodrama effectively without giving interpretations of the meaning of symptoms or behavior.

Variations on psychodrama or role-playing are widely used for job-training purposes. They have been incorporated into training programs in the health professions and in the business world for posts such as that of sales person, receptionist, and supervisor.

FAMILY THERAPY AND FAMILY GROUP THERAPY

Although working with the families of disturbed children was a common practice in child guidance clinics as long ago as the 1920s and 1930s, the practice of bringing the entire family or several families together for group therapy began in the 1950s. In 1958, Nathan Ackerman, a psychoanalyst who specialized in child development and had studied disturbed families, published in *The Psychodynamics of Family Life* the first description of psychotherapy of a whole family. Other family therapists, among them Jackson and his co-workers in Palo Alto, and Bowen and his group at the National Institutes of Health in Bethesda, had been working in similar ways. Most of these early family therapists had psychoanalytic training and used insight-oriented techniques. Several other approaches were evolving at that time, however, including some in which specific strategies were employed, such as directing the topics of family conversations or assigning specific behavior tasks (Haley, 1963).

Family therapy can be insight-oriented, process-oriented, or be-havioral-oriented. Some family therapists work exclusively with the entire family. Others will see individual family members in some sessions, the entire family in others, and sets of family members in still others. There have been efforts to evolve a theory of family development and family therapy, but no model that is acceptable to a majority of family therapists has yet emerged.

Nevertheless, most family therapists assume that personality dis-organization in any member is a function of disturbance through-out the family. Conversely, the disturbed behavior of one family member is seen to create disturbances in other family members as they attempt to cope with it. The symptoms thus generated in all members of the family are usually reflected in disturbed commu-nication. When the communication between family members is dominated by the disturbed relationships, or the family reaches the point where it is incapable of resolving difficulties, the entire family becomes the appropriate focus of therapy.

The therapist's role depends upon his conceptual model of psy-chotherapy. Some family therapists confront the family members with their behavior, in the hope of making them aware of what they are communicating indirectly and non-verbally, as well as di-rectly, to one another. Others try to develop family members' in-sight into their interactions by offering interpretations about aspects of their behavior that are unclear or unconscious. Most fam-ily therapists attempt to deal with the family as a unit rather than to direct their comments and other therapeutic interventions to individual members.

ENCOUNTER GROUPS

Encounter groups are both a very new development on the psycho-therapy scene and a very old way for groups of people to deal with problems—though it is probably not accurate to consider en-counter groups a form of psychotherapy, since they exist largely outside the traditional mental health care system. In fact the encounter group movement seems to represent a reaction against many traditional forms of therapy.

Encounter groups are usually brief, intensive, face-to-face interactions, not necessarily restricted to verbal communication. There is strong emphasis on openness, honesty, and expression of strong feelings. Self-disclosure and spontaneous, even physical, expressions of feeling are encouraged. Therapeutic goals range from those indistinguishable from goals of conventional psychotherapy to those of consciousness raising, greater self-expression, or simply the enjoyment of a warm, mutual experience.

According to Lieberman, Yalom, and Miles (1973), the forerunner of present-day encounter groups was a series of workshops conducted by Kurt Lewin in Connecticut in 1946 to train community leaders to reduce racial tensions. Participants in these workshops were assigned to small discussion groups to analyze what they had experienced in their own communities. Each group maintained records that were to be reviewed by the workshop staff in evening planning sessions, which were open to all other participants in that day's workshop. Both the content and the process in the discussion groups were reviewed during the evening meetings. Participants agreed that the evening meetings augmented their understanding of their own behavior and its impact on the community problems being discussed. The staff realized that they had discovered a training method in human relations, and subsequently organized annual summer laboratories under sponsorship of the National Training Laboratories (NTL), an organization founded by the staff of that first 1946 experiment.

As these training groups evolved, they became known as "T-groups" or sensitivity-training groups, and later as encounter groups. More and more people saw them as a way of achieving personal growth, development of one's full potential, or simply greater self-understanding. Encounter groups were increasingly used by professional psychotherapists but developed even more rapidly outside the mental health care system.

Although the original encounter groups developed by NTL tended to emphasize free and unstructured interactions without prescribed tasks for the group, in recent years encounter groups have often used *structured exercises*. In these exercises the leader intervenes in the group process to give a set of specific orders or prescriptions for behavior. These may include a variety of prescriptions for speech or action, such as setting up a psychodrama, instructing a number of group members to surround one member, who has been instructed to close his eyes and fall backward (considered an exercise in trust), or directing one group member to describe his feelings about another member. In *Joy* by Schutz (1967), a large number of structured exercises are described. Each exercise has a specific aim, such as to promote feelings of warmth, closeness, or trust; to alter the group interaction; to promote self-understanding; to encourage expression of feeling and self-disclosure; to strengthen the experience of feelings; to change feelings toward another member or toward the group.

Encounter group leaders who emphasize the authority inherent in the role of leader are most likely to use a large number of structured exercises.

The ten approaches to encounter groups studied by Lieberman, Yalom, and Miles are representative of the many existing varieties, some of which defy description. They will be reviewed briefly below.

T-group or sensitivity-training group
In this, the traditional NTL approach, the leader's role is to help members understand themselves and others through examining the interactional process going on in the group. The leader attempts to explain what is happening within the group. Accordingly, he may point out such things as cohesiveness or lack of it, the development of subgroups, and the scapegoating of a member. The aim is to raise the level of awareness each member has of such interactions in the T-group and in other groups he may enter. Some T-groups emphasize self-disclosure and give social reinforce-

ment for it. Others stress the expression of negative feelings, while still others devote their efforts to identifying and describing such interactions as attempts to exercise power or ways in which work is distributed when the group undertakes a task.

Gestalt therapy

In gestalt therapy, change is viewed as a process that takes place unconsciously but can be stimulated "by helping the individual get in touch with the primitive wisdom of the body." In a gestalt-oriented encounter group much emphasis is placed on strengthening the direct expression of feelings, both verbally and non-verbally, and on understanding what the body communicates about oneself non-verbally. Posture, gait, carriage or bearing, and gestures are thus interpreted as reflections of unconscious attitudes or feelings. Efforts are made to bring out any conflicting messages apparently being communicated by different parts of the body. Efforts are also made to act out feelings that have been held under control, suppressed, or previously unconscious. Leaders of gestalt therapy groups tend to rely heavily on structured exercises in the effort to accomplish these goals.

Transactional analysis

Transactional analysis was discussed in Chapter 5 and again earlier in this chapter as a type of process-oriented group therapy. It also has many characteristics of an encounter group.

Esalen eclectic

This approach was first described by Schutz, who introduced a large number of structured exercises into encounter groups in an effort to accelerate the development of closeness and the experience of feelings among group members. He also sought to free them from the usual social and physical inhibitions that limit the amount of contact in ordinary social groups. The group leader focuses on both the individuals in the group and the relations between them. Among the structured exercises used are those aimed at overcoming inhibitions by having members do things that are difficult or embarrassing for them. Others involve fantasy exercises (i.e., imagine that you are an animal) to be described aloud. Emphasis is on the immediate experience and the direct physical expression of feeling. Leaders tend to use a great deal of authority.

Personal growth (NTL groups, western style)
In this development of the T-group emphasis has shifted from the group itself to a Rogerian conception of the individual within the group, as described earlier in this chapter. As in Rogerian group therapy, the leader's attention centers on the expression of feeling by the group members. The major difference is that personal growth groups are meant not for the disturbed but for normal people who are seeking further personal development.

Synanon
The Synanon group, sometimes called the "Synanon Game," is quite different from other encounter groups. Its membership consists of some regulars and some who come occasionally or for only one or two sessions. There is no official leader, though experienced "game" players tend to become leaders for part or all of a given session. Each participant in a session sooner or later becomes the focus of one or more of the other members—usually the one playing the leader role. This person explores the behavior of the member in question, even to his dress, manner, or attitude, and attacks him on all such points. The supposition appears to be that if one is attacked in his weak spots long enough, he will grow stronger in them. Once the group session is over, the atmosphere quickly becomes warmly supportive. Those who participate are either members of Synanon, a residential self-help community for people with problems ranging from drug addiction to severe social maladjustment, and Synanon "life-stylers," those who do not live at Synanon but spend time there and take part in the Synanon Game.

Psychodrama

Lieberman and his associates consider psychodrama to be an encounter group in its own right, as well as an auxiliary technique in many other types of encounter groups.

Marathon

The marathon, or time-extended group meeting, is the most intensive encounter group of all. A marathon group meets for a long stretch of time—twelve, twenty-four, or even forty-eight hours—without pause. The group may meet only once, or the meeting may be repeated or followed by briefer encounter sessions. In some marathon groups members may take short sleep periods, but in others even this is discouraged, in the belief that prolonged contact and physical exhaustion accelerate and intensify the interaction between group members and the expression of feelings that are normally submerged. A high value is placed on self-expression, honesty, and aggressive confrontation between group members.

Psychoanalytically oriented groups

These are relatively conservative encounter groups led by psychoanalytically oriented clinicians, and often composed of students in the helping professions. They focus on the dynamics of an individual's responses to the group, viewed from the perspective of his own psychological development. Since they also emphasize often the learning of group dynamics, they are less emotionally charged and more didactic than the other groups.

Encountertapes (leaderless groups)

Leaderless groups are not uncommon in the encounter movement, though an unofficial leader usually emerges even in these groups. Elizabeth Brown has developed a set of tape recordings that a leaderless encounter group can play during each meeting. Marketed under the trade name "Encountertapes" by Bell and Howell, they have gained widespread use. The tapes contain instructions for a series of structured exercises, indicating when one exercise should stop and another begin. A leader's voice gives the instructions as well as some rather non-specific feedback, and generally "directs" the entire meeting. Group members are told to follow the tape's instructions, which include when to turn it off and on during the meeting.

This is hardly an all-inclusive account of the encounter groups that are arising in this fast-growing movement. Many groups draw on a combination of the approaches described above, in addition to others. Among the more imaginative variations are nude encounter groups, group encounters in heated swimming pools, and sexual-encounter groups.

PEER GROUPS OF PATIENTS WITH CHRONIC DISEASES

Since the days of Pratt's original work with tuberculosis patients in Boston, groups of patients suffering from the same chronic illness have been meeting to deal with their common problems. Alcoholics Anonymous is probably the best known. Another is the Ostomate Association, a national organization with many local chapters, whose members have had colostomies or ileostomies. They have been meeting for many years to share information about how to deal with their problems, to give warm support to each other, and often to hear instructive or inspirational speeches by invited lecturers. Recovery Inc., is a parallel group composed of the mentally ill. Peer groups of multiple sclerosis and cancer patients have also been formed.

Such groups can be an important adjunct to the rehabilitation of patients with chronic disease. They can increase self-esteem, improve morale, and help patients establish social relations when they have difficulty finding acceptance by those not ill or disabled. The groups may have a closed or open-ended membership, and be of extended or limited duration. Most peer groups for chronically ill patients are not psychotherapy groups in the usual sense. If there is a leader, his function is mainly to facilitate the interactional process rather than to conduct a therapy session. Such leader may serve also as a source of information or as a guide in focusing the group's attention on a common problem that the members can help each other solve.

REFERENCES

Berne, E. *Principles of Group Treatment.* New York: Oxford University Press, 1966.
Enelow, A. J., and Wexler, M. *Psychiatry in the Practice of Medicine.* New York: Oxford University Press, 1966.
Goldstein, A., and Wolpe, J. "Behavior Therapy in Groups." In *Comprehensive Group Therapy*, by H. I. Kaplan, and B. J. Sadock. Baltimore: Williams and Wilkins, 1971.
Haley, J. *Strategies of Psychotherapy.* New York: Grune and Stratton, 1963.
Johnson, J. A. *Group Therapy: A Practice Approach.* New York: McGraw-Hill, 1963.
Kaplan, H. I., and Sadock, B. J. "Structural Interactional Group Psychotherapy." In *Comprehensive Group Therapy*.
Levine, M. *Psychotherapy in Medical Practice.* New York: Macmillan, 1948.
Lieberman, M. A.; Yalom, I. D.; and Miles, M. B. *Encounter Groups: First Facts.* New York: Basic Books, 1973.
Moreno, J. L. "Psychodrama." In *Comprehensive Group Therapy*.
Sadock, B. J. "Group Psychotherapy." In *Comprehensive Textbook of Psychiatry II*, by A. Freedman, H. I. Kaplan, and B. J. Sadock. Baltimore: Williams and Wilkins, 1975.
Schutz, W. C. *Firo: A Three-Dimensional Theory of Interpersonal Behavior.* New York: Rinehart, 1958.
———. *Joy.* New York: Grove Press, 1967.
Wolpe, J. *The Practice of Behavior Therapy.* 2nd ed. New York: Pergamon Press, 1973.
Yalom, I. *The Theory and Practice of Group Psychotherapy.* New York: Basic Books, 1970.

INDEX